HOLLY

PROTECT WHAT YOU CHERISH

BY GUARDING WHAT YOU'VE BEEN GIVEN

Learning to use your
weakness as a weapon

Protect What You Cherish

Copyright ® 2025 by Holly Myers
Published by UNITED HOUSE Publishing
All rights reserved. No portion of this book may be reproduced or shared in any form - electronic, printed, photocopied, recording, or by any information storage or retrieval system, without prior written permission from the publisher. The use of short quotations is permitted.

ISBN - 978-1-952840-67-8

UNITED HOUSE Publishing Clarkston, Michigan
info@unitedhousepublishing.com www.unitedhousepublishing.com

Author Photograph: Gwendolyn Vanegas Photography

Cover Design: Ariel Faulkner; arielcfaulkner@gmail.com
Interior Design: Talitha McGuinness; talitha@unitedhousepublishing.com

Printed in the United States of America 2025 - First Edition

SPECIAL SALES:
Most UNITED HOUSE books are available at special quantity discounts when purchased in bulk by corporations, organizations, and special interest groups. For more information, please email orders@unitedhousepublishing.com.

DEDICATION

To Richard, Rebekah, Rachel and my new son-in-law, Austin. Also my mom, dad, Jenna Mason, family, and all my dear friends who have walked through a lot with me and chose to stay.

I cherish you more than anything.

Protect What You Cherish

I will never forget the day that **Protect What You Cherish** was birthed into Holly's heart. I can still feel the sting in my arm after getting an "ah ha" moment slap when it all clicked in her mind, her calling to write this book was clear. Holly is someone that seeks the Lord whole heartedly and genuinely. She is someone who desires to know and understand God's word and share every bit of it with others and I know this book will do exactly that. I can say these things about Holly with such confidence because I have witnessed it myself for the past 15 years of my life. I have seen the literal blood, sweat, and tears that have come from a life of obedience to God's call! This book will draw you into a deeper desire to know God's will for your life and give you such a hunger for His word! I am so thankful to call Holly my best friend, and I have been waiting a long time to finally say, I endorse this book!

Ariel Faulkner
Pastor's wife, Unbound Ministry leadership

I am honored to have the opportunity to write an endorsement for my best friend's book. Holly is a dedicated and passionate cheerleader for helping girls and women discover that true freedom can only be found in Christ.

One of the things I admire most about Holly is her unwavering faith and her willingness to share her own vulnerabilities and struggles in order to point others towards Jesus. Her authenticity and transparency make her message all the more powerful. Her genuine heart for empowering other women to break free from the chains of bondage and walk in the freedom that only comes from a relationship with Christ is evident in everything she does.

Protect What You Cherish

Holly's adventurous spirit and contagious enthusiasm for life shine through in every word. Holly's words are reflections of a heart that is deeply committed to leading others towards Christ. Her heart and message are sure to impact and transform lives for the glory of God.

Thank you, Holly, for sharing your heart and your wisdom with the world. You are truly a gift to all who know you, including myself. I love you, sweet friend.

Nicki Carnes
Pastor's wife/Ministry leader
Hope Church, Augusta, Georgia

Of the many things I've grown to know and love about Holly Myers is her fierce, determined, unwavering focus on freedom, a freedom in God that has been purchased through pain, vulnerability, and a cherished love of others she so deeply marks with her compassion. She is momma Bear! She knows the struggles, the pitfalls, the yokes of comparing yourself and how to break free! She reveals the weaknesses of her own life and the ones we all want to hide, yet she loves relentlessly. Her calling to see all those around her embrace freedom and acceptance is as liberating as the bird that's set free from a cage. I pray when you read her book you can begin your own journey of freedom.

We have escaped like a bird from the snare of the fowlers, the trap is broken and we have escaped. Our help is in the name of the Lord, who made heaven and earth. Psalm 124:7

Deborah Lambert
Bible Teacher (Holly's Mentor)

By Guarding What You've Been Given

In *Protect What You Cherish*,
Holly Myers delivers a powerful message to women everywhere who have felt the pressures of the world weighing them down. With vulnerability and authenticity, Holly shares her own journey towards freedom and identity in Christ. This book is a must-read for any woman who is tired of striving for acceptance and ready to embrace the truth of who she is in God's eyes. Holly's words are a reminder that true freedom can only be found in Jesus Christ. I highly recommend this book to all women who are ready to protect what they cherish and walk in the freedom that is rightfully theirs.

Natalie Grant
Recording Artist & Philanthropist

———————————————

Holly Myers is the type of gal who will have you laughing through tears, claiming the truths of Scripture through hardship, raising your hands in worship through fear, and clinging to confidence in the character of God when you're down and out. I know this because she has inspired me personally to do all these things. ***Protect What You Cherish*** is a labor of a love letter to the Church, reminding her to guard the "good deposit that was entrusted" to you and me by the Holy Spirit. This message and this messenger will help you rise to the occasion for such a time as this.

Lauren Alexander
Bible teacher

———————————————

Freedom is the song of Holly's heart. From intentionality to words of wisdom, Holly's desire to see people living an untethered, unchained life of freedom in Christ makes her not only the apple of the King's eyes, but also as an example freedom for so many others.

Her testimony is powerful, and being able to watch her life's calling beautifully written out for others' encouragement, strength, and wisdom is just another reminder of God's hands of freedom in her life.

Holly's words are never minced and are always a straight arrow to Christ and His freedom.

Rachael Rushing
Unbound Ministry leadership

FOREWARD

In September 1995, I moved up to the foothills of the Appalachian mountains. It was there at the prettiest little liberal arts college nestled in the one traffic light town of Mars Hill that God revealed Himself to me in a BIG way. At first I didn't quite recognize it was Him. I was a naive freckle-faced freshman education major from sunny Florida and was living away from home for the first time ever. I was hundreds of miles from home and working on earning a college degree while also searching for purpose, validation, love, and friendship like many other girls my age. I had friends back home that I had known since I was a baby and had grown up in the same church for my entire 18 years of life. I had loving, supportive parents and had a great high school experience. I had earned a scholarship to attend Mars Hill College and I definitely wanted to keep up the image that I had it all together and that I knew what I was doing and where I was going. That couldn't have been further from the truth. However, like so many young college students I was searching. I longed to find friends in this new phase of life that would push me like never before. I wanted friends that would share the same longings and desires for a real, meaningful relationship with Jesus. I wanted friends that I could share the good and the bad moments with without any fear of judgement. I wanted friends that I could be completely vulnerable with and that would lovingly encourage and support me. I wanted someone to help me to be the best version of myself and help me to be all that God was calling me to be. I couldn't articulate it at the time, but God knew my heart. And God sent me Holly Myers.

Protect What You Cherish

"The Father knows what you need before you ask him."
Matthew 6:8 NIV

I was immediately drawn to Holly when I met her my freshman year. She was the prettiest girl I had ever seen. She was sweet, funny, outgoing, and kind. She was on our school's award-winning clogging team which was very impressive. (And when I learned later, being a child of the 80's myself, that she had been on Star Search AND HeeHaw, I thought she was the coolest person I had ever met). She was silly and fun and we laughed constantly. It was amazing the way God began growing this beautiful friendship right from the start and neither of us knew how special or impactful it would be. As we spent more time together and got to know one another even more, we started sharing more about our lives. I realized that as perfect as Holly seemed to me on the outside, she was struggling just like I was with self loathing and self doubt and hiding the wounds of past hurts. And there was such a feeling of comfort and safety like I've never felt before as I slowly began sharing my insecurities and struggles with her. We began encouraging each other and lifting each other up and my burdens felt lighter the more time we spent together. We also shared the same desire to grow closer to God and as Holly overcame so many things she was battling, her life and her testimony taught me about the true freedom found in Jesus Christ. I began to let go of so many thoughts and feelings that were holding me back and began leaning in even more to my relationship with my Savior.

It's been many years since our college days, and our friendship has continued to grow through the years. We've watched each other walk through so much joy and sadness, births and deaths, carefree days and difficult ones, and all the ups and downs of life. I continue to be amazed by the way God has worked in and through Holly. He has loved her, changed her, redeemed her and used her for His purpose. She has spoken so much truth into my life and into the lives of countless women and girls who have struggled with the same self-doubt and insecurities that we did. She has opened up her heart and allowed her pain and her difficult journey to inspire and encourage others.

"As iron sharpens iron, so one person sharpens another."
Proverbs 27:17 NIV

I know Holly so well. Every word in this book comes from a sincere heart that wants each person to experience the freedom and joy that's only found in Jesus. As her friend for almost twenty years, I can honestly say, I have seen firsthand the way God has moved in her life. I have seen the way God has changed her. I pray that as you read this book you will not only feel the sincerity of her words, but that you will also be drawn to experience the transformative, life-changing power and love of Jesus Christ in your life.

"To God be the glory forever and ever. Amen."
Galatians 1:5 GNT

Rebekah Deaton
College best friend (also current best friend)

Protect What You Cherish

By Guarding What You've Been Given

Freedom is messy and beautiful.

As I sat out on a balcony in Haiti at the beginning of 2021, I was overwhelmed by the mountains. I could see hills upon hills in the distance. The sun was so bright, and I could hear birds flying from tree to tree. However, I couldn't see the valleys. I knew they were there because I had seen the faces that lived in those valleys. I heard the cries of sweet, hungry children that carried for what seemed like miles away. Just like those deep valleys in Haiti, there are also deep valleys we walk through. This book came from a lot of valleys. It was birthed from seasons of change, heartache, and desperation. Insecurities drove me to believe lies about myself, my calling, my ministry, my friendships, and my future.

I don't know when it happened, but something changed. I no longer allow insecurities to enslave me by allowing my weaknesses to become the very weapons I used to slay the enemy's tactics to keep me in bondage. Freedom came out of that fight, and, oh my goodness, it was a messy but beautiful journey that forever changed me.

It is for freedom that Christ has set us free. Stand firm, then, and do not let yourselves be burdened again by a yoke of slavery.
Galatians 5:1, NIV

If there is one thing I am certain of, it is that freedom was given to us by Jesus, and bondage is from the enemy.

The thief's purpose is to steal and kill and destroy. My purpose is to give them a rich and satisfying life.
John 10:10, NLT

Protect What You Cherish

Jesus wants you to walk in freedom in all areas of your life. He wants to satisfy every longing you have. That means your callings, your dreams, your relationships, friendships, and ministry, and in your day-to-day life. The enemy's strategy, however, is to keep you in chains. So, knowing this, what do we do?

We fight.

How do we fight, you ask?

Sweet friends, we use the weaknesses that have kept us quiet and afraid to move for far too long. We worship louder, serve God with our whole hearts, surrender every ounce of self, and then get stronger than ever. It is time to move forward with our heads held high, with our hearts positioned to receive, and our feet ready to move in whatever direction God is sending us and calling us to, regardless of what the destination may be.

> *But He said to me, "My grace is sufficient for you, for my power is made perfect in weakness." Therefore I will boast all the more gladly about my weaknesses, so that Christ's power may rest on me. That is why, for Christ's sake, I delight in weaknesses, in insults, in hardships, in persecutions, in difficulties. For when I am weak, then I am strong.*
> 2 Corinthians 12:9-10, NLT

Will you take a moment to open your hands (palms open) and ask God to do a new thing in and through you? Will you pray for the words on every page to stir, heal, and bring about change so you can fight from a different place? Whether you are high on the mountain or deep in the valley, you have what it takes in Jesus' name to keep going and spread Jesus's hope from right where you are to the ends of the earth. If you like to journal, use this moment to write it out; if not, speak it out loud.

Are you ready?

Okay, good. **LET'S GO!**

By Guarding What You've Been Given

Protect What You Cherish

CHAPTER 1

"Guard your heart like your life depends on it because it does."[1]
Jackie Hill Perry

Guard Your Heart

I love bears.

I love learning random facts about bears, from what they eat to where they sleep to how they sound when they are mad or sense danger. This bear obsession is only a few years old, and it all started with a dream.

I woke up one morning, and I was so confused by what I had dreamed, yet it seemed so real at the time. In my dream, I was driving on the interstate, and all of the cars around me suddenly started pulling over and stopping abruptly. It was one of those slam-on-the-brakes-almost-causing-me-to-wreck types of stops. I was looking to see what they were all looking at.

A mama bear and her cubs were coming up over the hill. I remember thinking in my dream: *all this for wanting to see a bear?* I also remember having no fear. Then I woke up. I thought about that bear all morning. As I went to have a coffee date that same day, my friend handed me a mug that had a bear on it. I immediately thought, hmm, I wonder what God is trying to teach me.

Fast forward a few months, and I again dreamed about a few different scenarios, all involving a bear. One dream was about a bear chasing a predator to save her cub. I also dreamed about a bear knocking over anything and everything in its path on the way up a huge hill. I dreamed about a bear going into a huge waterfall to catch fish, and it was as if I was always right in the midst of what the bear was doing, but never once was I afraid. The weird and also amazing part about these dreams is that they would come back to my mind with such clarity. I remember standing in worship at my church on a Sunday, and as we sang "Reckless Love" by Cory Asbury, the imagery of that bear going up that mountain, moving everything in its path, went through my mind. It was an image that will forever be etched into my brain.

Okay, so now you see there is a theme in my dream life and a growing curiosity and obsession about bears. Little by little, God kept revealing sweet messages to me, but it wasn't until months later that I was standing in worship at a summer camp, and God clearly revealed to me what He was trying to say so loudly to my soul. Up until that point, I had only seen the bear wandering, protecting, and seeking food in my dreams. On this particular night, as I was standing in worship, we were singing "Spirit of the Living God," and with my eyes closed and my palms open, I saw this ginormous bear stand up in my mind. I could almost feel the dirt flying around this bear. I could hear the noises coming from him, and I heard God say so clearly to my spirit, "Holly, it's time to stand in your calling." It wrecked me. I immediately Googled, "Why do bears stand up?" (Thank goodness for Google! Am I right?)

I found out that bears can see, hear, and smell better while standing up than when they are down on all four legs.

Something begins to change when we stand firm in the truth of God's Word and fix our eyes on Him alone. The things that you were once chasing after, like approval or the desire to be seen, can suddenly become a threat and begin to shape you. The beauty of God's Word brings clarity so that we can know what or even who needs to be removed from our lives.
One fun fact that most people know about mama bears is that they will fight anything for their cubs. They will remove whatever

is a threat or at least fight with everything to protect what is theirs.

I get it, Mama Bear.

There have been things in my life that I cared for and guarded with every ounce of my being (which I will share a little about in each chapter). Things like unhealthy thought patterns, friendships that made me feel worse about myself, and binge eating behind closed doors just to feel better about myself. I guarded all of it because I believed, deep down, that this was the only way to live—in chains, in bondage, and far from ever experiencing victory and freedom in my life.

My youngest daughter, Rachel, went off to college at the end of 2020, and before she ever received an acceptance letter, she had her Amazon cart full of how she would decorate her dorm room. She had pictures of decor down to the bedspread and lamps ready to go. At the end of the year, when it was about a month out from her leaving to come home, I commented one night that she should go ahead and start taking the things off her wall and packing them up, and you would have thought I had said something so offensive. She said, "Mom, no way! I don't want to have blank walls for an entire month!"

Goodness, isn't that how we are at times within our minds? We can't stand for our minds to not be filled with something, even if it keeps us in bondage. We desire to be comfortable, and we desire to be seen, so we begin to fill the space.

Wherever we dwell, we decorate. And when we decorate, we get attached. And when we get attached, it's harder to let go.

For example, if you dwell in an "I am not worthy of love" state of mind, you will eventually begin decorating that space. You will begin to strive to be liked, or you will lay your heart down over and over until you are completely addicted to the approval of people. I want you to finish this book with new decor hanging in your mind. I want you to have a new perspective and, ultimately, a changed heart towards your perceived weaknesses. God loves you, and your story of pain has a purpose.

Sweet friend, **your wreckage has the power to become someone else's rescue**. This theme of protecting what you cherish by guarding what you have been given is near and dear to my heart. I am still learning what it means to cherish, guard, and protect the beautiful things God has placed in my care this season and in this generation, and I can't wait to share with you how I am doing just that while encouraging you to do the same.

I love to look up word definitions because they help me understand a word's meaning even more. So humor me . . .

Webster defines the following:

Protect: to cover[2]

Cherish: to hold dear[3]

Guard: a defense[4]

We tend to protect the things that keep us enslaved rather than choosing to guard the God-given things that propel us into freedom.

I asked myself repeatedly what God actually gave me to protect, and one by one, I listed them on a piece of paper. From that list, I began to really seek the Bible for the "how" part.
I started with my heart.

If your heart is broken, wounded, bruised, or numb, lean in because that means you are in need of something from Your Creator, and He has something new for you.

*I will give you a new heart and put a new spirit in you;
I will remove from you your heart of stone and give you a
heart of flesh.*

By Guarding What You've Been Given

Ezekiel 36:26, ESV

Before you dive deeper into this book, take a few moments in prayer. Maybe that means you need to change your posture, get on your knees, or hold your palms up (like I did), and ask God to reveal to you what you're hiding behind and even protecting.

Could it be pain that was caused by someone else?

Could it be unforgiveness keeping you in a place of constant bitterness?

Could it be insecurities keeping you from dreaming?

Could it be unbelief?

Before you move forward in using your weaknesses as a weapon, you have to stand back up, and your first step is to surrender. If you fight against darkness with insecurities, then you're essentially trying to fight with lies, because insecurities are rooted in lies. But if you are weak because you have found yourself wounded or not strong in an area, remember that God can use those things to bring forth something mighty through you, because "His power is made perfect in your weakness" (2 Corinthians 12:9).

If you are weary today, it's ok, sweet friend; I promise God will strengthen you.

So take a new grip with your tired hands and strengthen your weak knees.
Hebrews 12:12, NLT

It's time to protect what you cherish by guarding what you have been given. It is time to cherish *new* things while God redeems and makes new things in you. It is time to guard from a new stance because you are victorious.

Protect What You Cherish

Have you ever watched a movie over and over, and before long, you're quoting it everywhere you go? My husband, Richard, and I married the summer before our senior year in college, and we were poor and in love. We couldn't afford cable, but we had a TV with a VHS player on the front of it. Every single night, we watched the movie "The Fugitive" with Harrison Ford. If the movie plays even now, I can visualize the entire movie without watching one scene.

One of my favorite quotes of the movie is this:

"Well, think me up a cup of coffee and a chocolate doughnut with some of those little sprinkles on top, while you're thinking."[5]

Y'all, twenty-five years later, I say that every single time Richard says the words, "I am thinking." The truth is our hearts are filled with such deceit, and if we aren't careful, our hearts lead our minds and feet into places we were never meant to go. *We begin to repeat what we know, and if we only know and believe the lies of the enemy or the deceit within our hearts, we will eventually make it a pattern in our lives.*

Our thoughts help steer our feet, and it starts with the condition of our hearts.

How do you protect your heart if you don't cherish it?

The answer is you won't protect it.

When someone has a heart attack, they almost always completely change their eating habits, because they are so scared that the next time could be fatal. The doctor removes the blockages so that blood can flow easily through the arteries, doing the job it was created to do. When build-up forms because of fatty foods or lack of exercise, the heart grows weak, and it has to work harder, causing it to weaken more and eventually stop.

By Guarding What You've Been Given

The buildup of sin, disobedience, and unhealthy emotions blocking our hearts will always cause us to work harder. Before we know it, we spiritually begin to slow down, weaken, and eventually stop moving toward Jesus or doing the things He has called us to do.

I don't know if you are like me, but y'all, laundry is truly my arch nemesis. I hate it. I will throw a load in the washer and then a load in the dryer, and when the dryer stops, I usually complain all the way there. I know that loud buzzing noise reminds me that the laundry needs to be folded and put away. Frequently, it goes from the dryer to my bedroom floor, and then three loads later, I usually can't find anything, and I end up yelling at my kids for stealing my clothes. It's a vicious cycle. Please tell me if anyone else can relate.

The same thing happens when my heart gets filled with all the ugly. Whether that is comparison, envy, or dislike of someone, you better believe every area of my life reflects those things. My attitude towards things like my body started with seeing every imperfection when I looked in the mirror. Before long, my mouth would put down my body by saying things like, "I hate my body." I could also see my attitude shifting in how I responded to my kids or resisted my calling and my dreams. Overall, my inward mess was coming out in every area of my life, and it wasn't pretty.

The ugly reality is that no matter how hard you work to maintain an image or to project and protect what God never meant to be, you will always work harder, yet never become satisfied. Did you know the Bible mentions the word "heart" over 800 times (Strong's Exhaustive Concordance of the Bible)? I believe so many people see a heart and immediately equate it with mushy feelings of love, marriage, desire, and attraction. From kindergarten through the fifth grade, we hung hearts in our classrooms and sent Valentines with hearts on them, so it's no wonder we think that way. But the word "heart," from a Biblical perspective, is so much more and so much deeper. It represents the core of who we are.

> *"The human heart is the most deceitful of all things, and desperately wicked. Who really knows how bad it is?*
> Jeremiah 17:9, NLT

The more you understand that the core of every decision you make is coming from the depth of your heart, the more you understand you have to let go of your desires, because it's those desires that pollute everything else. When we ask God to take our hearts and make them new, He doesn't rearrange what's in there. He removes anything that has the potential to block His love from you receiving it.

We can't have one foot in freedom and one foot in bondage; that just means you're still in bondage. It's like fighting with your hands held behind your back, and one hit from the enemy may cause you to slip, but a harder fall is inevitable.

> *Who can say, "I have cleansed my heart; I am pure and free from sin?"*
> Proverbs 20:9, NLT

When I hit forty, reading was suddenly a chore because I couldn't see the pages clearly anymore. When I first started needing glasses, I would buy a pair at the dollar store so that I could toss them and buy more when they got scratched. But when I finally invested in a twenty-dollar pair from Amazon, suddenly, I kept them in a case and would clean them because I didn't want them to get scratched.

When you cherish something, you want it clean, not dirty.

If you watch porn, it will affect your heart.

If you have sex outside of marriage, it will affect your heart.

By Guarding What You've Been Given

If you gossip, it will affect your heart.

If you are numb to the things of God's Word, it will affect your heart.

The list could go on and on because those are the behaviors of an unsurrendered heart. Those things don't define you, but they show the areas of your heart that need attention before one decision based on a dirty heart turns into a season of regret. Did you know bears have excellent memories? I was reading about them online recently. Mama bears and cubs grieve deeply when separated. For weeks at a time, they squeal and cry because they can feel the separation. Just thinking about the sweet little cub squealing for his mama hurts my heart.

Y'ALL, I can't.

But can we just stop and think about what that would look like if we longed for Jesus like that? Not out of guilt or striving but because we long to be in His presence. I love that mama bears love their cubs so much they will risk their lives for them, but even more, I love that Jesus chose to lay down His life for you and me to experience fullness, freedom, satisfaction, and completion that will only ever come from Him.

So, how do you protect your heart?

You surrender it.

You ask God to cleanse it. You get up tomorrow and do it again, and then do it again the next day and the day after until the moment you walk into Heaven. Sweet friend, this world is polluted, and the enemy wants to toxify your heart, but it's not his heart to mess with. **The devil can't taunt you with what he doesn't own.** If you are a believer, your heart belongs to God—every single part of it.

It's time to stand your ground.

So, my dear brothers and sisters, be strong and immovable. Always work enthusiastically for the Lord, for you know that nothing you do for the Lord is ever useless.
1 Corinthians 15:58, NLT

I love this verse because it says to be strong and immovable. My brother was the strongest person I knew when I was a kid. If I had friend issues or boyfriend issues, I would always threaten people with my big brother. Clay was always in my corner. He was always willing to fight my battles for me; all I had to do was ask him. I believe protecting our hearts is vital for our walk with Jesus because God steps in and fights for us when our hearts are weakened.

The Lord himself will fight for you. Just stay calm.
Exodus 14:14, NLT

Just like a mama bear standing to her feet to look to see what is coming towards her babies, God can see the threats coming your way when you can't, and He will fight on your behalf. I can't say much more about how important it is to guard your heart, but oh my goodness, friend, everything you do for the rest of your time on earth flows out of the condition of your heart. Proverbs 4:23 (ESV) is my favorite verse concerning our hearts. It says, "Guard your heart above all else, for it determines the course of your life."

Those words. . . "above all else."

That means you guard your heart **above** the guy you desire to be in a relationship with who pushes and stirs up emotions in you to give in to being physical with him. That means when your body is screaming "yes," you say NO, regardless of how you feel or what you desire. It means standing your ground and being immovable in God's truth. Sadly, it also means you may need to walk away. That means instead of running to food, porn, or any other temporary fix, **you choose the holy way out.** Because in choosing the holy way out, you protect your heart. The holy way is sometimes the hardest because there will always be a sacrifice in order. Some of you may need to walk away from that physical relationship. Or maybe it's telling someone that you have an addiction and admitting it is your first step to surrendering and stepping into holiness. I get it; holy is hard, but it provides a covering only God can do for you.

Above all else, it is a picture where nothing comes in direct competition with your heart being fully surrendered. You choose Jesus every time. Our feelings can mess with our hearts and even cause us to believe that somehow they are from God. Even though that is so far from the truth, we often give in to our desires. What was once clear becomes a blurry line of questioning.

I remember being in college and not knowing why I believed what I believed. I took a Christian ethics class, and at the beginning of the semester, my professor asked everyone to stand in the middle of the classroom. He said, "If you are pro-life, stand on this side, and if you are pro-choice, stand on this side." The entire class stood on the pro-life side. At the end of the semester, he did the same exercise, except this time, the class was more than split down the middle. Most of the class had shifted to the opposite side they once opposed. We heard stories that pulled on our heartstrings. We heard stories that made us think from a different perspective, and I had to dig deep into trying to figure out why I believed what I believed.

The enemy will always blur the lines of truth because if he can get us to shift our eyes off of truth and onto our feelings, then he is halfway there.

Our feelings will always steer us in the direction of our desires. If our desires aren't guarded in the context of God's holiness, then it will cause us to make decisions based on the opposite of holiness.

Protect What You Cherish

I want to tell you a story about something that happened to me as a kid. Have you ever heard of Keds? The cute little white shoes that were super popular back in the 80s. I am pretty sure Jennifer Grey wore some in the movie ***Dirty Dancing***, but I remember all the girls had them in my class, and I wanted some so badly. There was a girl I was friends with who had several pairs, and she knew that I had a "fake" pair. So, we cut off the back of one of her pairs of Keds and super glued the label to my fake pair. I wore them, and no one knew but my friend and me. Though it worked, I constantly worried about that dumb label coming off. I was trying to wear a pair of non-Keds posing as Keds, and if one person had looked inside, they would have seen that what was inside did not match the label glued to the back.

The same goes for the sin we leave lurking in the hidden corners of our hearts. We often try so hard to create this identity on the outside, yet our hearts look nothing like who we are trying to be. We have this false illusion that if we pose as one thing, somehow we won't be rejected, forgotten, or feel shame, and that is not true at all because behind every lie is the father of lies himself.

You are of your father the devil, and your will is to do your father's desires. He was a murderer from the beginning, and does not stand in the truth, because there is no truth in him. When he lies, he speaks out of his own character, for <u>he is a liar and the father of lies.</u>
(emphasis mine)
John 8:44, ESV

Just like our physical hearts need to be protected by the things we put into our bodies, the same goes for our hearts when it comes to our spiritual lives. The saying "garbage in, garbage out" is true, and we must be aware of not only what we are letting in but also the condition of our hearts in all seasons. So, let's take a few moments to reflect, shall we?

By Guarding What You've Been Given

Before we move on to the next thing that I believe we are to guard with everything, we have to start with our hearts.

Take a moment to reflect on the hidden corners, the things you stuffed down deep, hoping never to deal with again. God's holiness exposes those areas, and it's not to make us feel shame but to heal us. **We can't heal what we aren't willing to surrender.** God's grace will cover every bit, but you have to lay it before Him.

What is it that is coming into direct competition with your heart?

Choose to pray and ask for forgiveness.

Repent and ask God to walk away or let go.

Cry it out (you know, one of those ugly cry moments).

But whatever you do, don't choose to do **nothing.**

Protecting what you cherish starts with guarding what you have been given, and I believe that, with everything in me, our hearts are where we have to start.

Before you move into Chapter 2, let's take a quick inventory of your heart's condition.

One of the things I text the girls and women I mentor often is this question: "How are your heart and mind?" I truly believe that allowing people to hear where our hearts and minds are highlights and often exposes where we truly are. I can tell people all day that I am "okay," but when people who truly know me see a certain demeanor or my face in some settings, I can almost know I am going to get a text or a phone call asking about what's really going on in my life. I have lied straight to people's faces about where my mind and heart were simply because I didn't want to admit it or even deal with it. It's like that chore you hate the most, hahaha.

Protect What You Cherish

I remember when I was in college, I sometimes waited until the night before something was due in classes I didn't like because I didn't want to do the work attached to subjects that bored me or I didn't enjoy. At the end of the semester, I would find myself cramming for exams or doing make-up work because the bad grades had caught up with me. Looking back, why did I not just do the hard work upfront? It was because it was truly UNBEARABLE. Okay, that was a little dramatic, but I hated math, biology, and anything that required me to exercise the parts of my brain that I was not good at using. But on the other hand, if I was sitting in a social work class, religion class, or a fun tennis class, I was striving for that A+. I enjoyed learning and exploring the things I was good at.

Let me free you up a little. The heart transformation isn't on you. It starts with allowing God to have your heart fully, and then, one by one, He removes the pieces that don't reflect Him. He redeems the areas where you keep holding on to bitterness or unforgiveness, and He transforms your mind and heart moment by moment to reflect His goodness, His mercy, and His unconditional grace. Not once, but over and over and over. The hard part is opening up to let Him fully have access. I don't know if you're like me, but I often feel like opening up those complex parts is daunting. I tend to see the mess and not the potential of what follows the cleansing. I spend time covering, escaping, or adding to the mess. I know that the moment I shift my perspective, walls begin to come down, as do the expectations of what should be. It is time to let your guard down and give Him an all-access pass to every corner of your heart.

> ***My son, give me your heart***
> ***and let your eyes delight in my ways***
> Proverbs 23:26, NIV

Below, you will see a blank space, and I want you to either write below or grab your own personal journal and take a few moments to write out your unfiltered thoughts about where your heart and mind are right now in this season. Then, take a few moments to sit with the Lord. He wants your heart more than anything because when your heart is tucked away in Him, you delight in His ways. Let this truth become a new anthem over your mind. Write it on a Post-it note (I tell everyone to do this). Stick it on the background of your phone. Highlight it in your bible, pray it, and remember that *your heart is not too far gone*.

God is a God that truly makes ALL THINGS NEW.

Sweet Friend . . .

How is your heart?

How is your mind?

Protect What You Cherish

By Guarding What You've Been Given

CHAPTER 2

"Hate is too great a burden to bear. It injures the hater more than it injures the hated."[6]
Coretta Scott King

Guard your body
Guard your mind

The first time I binged on food and felt deep regret, to the point I realized I had a problem, was when I pulled through the drive-thru and ordered an entire dozen Krispy Kreme donuts. I was having a terrible day, and honestly, I have no idea why. In my mind, I thought if I could just eat a donut or two, I would feel better emotionally. So, one donut turned into three, and before I knew it, I had devoured the entire dozen. I pulled over and vomited on the side of the road. I truly hated myself at that moment, and I wish that were the end. *It wasn't . . .*

Years of ordering salads in front of people and eating whatever I could get my hands on behind closed doors is how I dealt with the hatred I had toward my body.

I hated my past.
I hated my thighs.
I hated my double chin.
I hated my frizzy hair.
I hated my calves.
I hated my arm fat.
I hated my body in dresses.
I hated my body in shorts.
I hated that my friendships were shallow.

Protect What You Cherish

The reality was that I couldn't be who God had called and designed me to be if I hated the body He designed for me to fulfill my purpose. In Matthew 22, it is clear what we are to do while in this world:

> *Jesus replied, "'You must love the Lord your God with all your heart, all your soul, and all your mind." This is the first and greatest commandment. A second is equally important: 'Love your neighbor as yourself.'"*
> Matthew 22:37-39, NLT

Guarding your mind and heart is vital to fulfilling God's call. However, look at verse 39. It reads, "A second is equally important. To Love your neighbor as yourself."

The truth is that I didn't love myself. Therefore, the love I showed others for years was always guarded. I convinced myself it was genuine, but it wasn't because it couldn't have been. For example, when trying to serve or do anything for people, whether for a birthday or just trying to help, it was often tainted because of how I was trying to project myself. I presented as though I cared deeply, but honestly, my self-hatred kept me from connecting fully because I had to guard that part of me. That alone could keep a wedge between me and intimacy with others.

Do you remember being in elementary school, and the teacher would pick two captains for the class kickball game? Just thinking about it makes my palms sweat. I was never picked first. I hated that feeling. I also hated it for the one standing alone at the end. It breaks my heart for several reasons, but one of those is that for many, including myself, this is where rejection takes root in our hearts. The teacher meant nothing by it. In fact, she was trying to create a fun game of kickball, but for someone who didn't already feel seen by her daddy, it was just another reminder that who I was wasn't good enough.

By Guarding What You've Been Given

I have always loved reflecting on the story of David in the Bible. Did you know that David wasn't even considered for king by his own father? But he was ordained and anointed by God before man chose him. That story blows my mind every time I read it, but it also reminds me that nothing can stop God's anointing on my life unless I disobey.

1 Samuel Chapter 16 says this:

Then Samuel asked, "Are these all the sons you have?" "There is still the youngest, "Jesse replied. "But he's out in the fields watching the sheeps and the goats."Send for him at once." Samuel said "we will not sit down to eat until he arrives."
1 Samuel 16:11, NLT

I believe that someone is holding this book in their hands. And you have tears streaming down your face because it's not a childhood kickball game that has you weepy. It's true that you walk through the halls of your schools every day, and no one sees or talks to you. You're the mom who has no interaction with adults, and you feel unseen and never chosen by others. You're the girl who hopes and waits for that guy to notice you, yet he walks by you, never looking your way. I wish I could create deep friendships for you, make that boy see your beauty, or fill your planner up with sweet interactions with others, but I can't. Just like you, I have sat in my car, bedroom, and kitchen table with tears streaming down my face because I have not only felt unseen but also believed that God, along with everyone else, was intentionally not choosing me. I blamed my past mistakes. I blamed the boy who broke my heart. I blamed the friendships that seemed safe but were the opposite of that. I blamed many people, but ultimately, it was a ME issue. It was an issue of hate. Hating myself had become a poison to my soul.

Chapter 1 discussed guarding your heart and how starting

there creates a clean slate for God to rebuild and renew what He has already begun in you. I promise He still wants to use you even though you don't love yourself. He does, however, want you to see that in Him, you are beautiful.

In this chapter, I want you to ask yourself this question:

Do I love what God has created?

In fact, take a moment and look at yourself in the mirror. Do you immediately see all the imperfections? Do you hate seeing your reflection? Do you wish you could change the shape of your face? Do you wish God would have redesigned what He has already deemed a masterpiece? If you answered yes to any of those, please hear me say you are not alone. A billion-dollar industry is out there to help us with every insecurity outside the body. If we have a zit, we buy concealer. If we see a pop of gray, we run to the salon for color. If we don't like a picture, we can download an app and make ourselves look skinnier and have whiter teeth. It blows my mind when I think about how real this idea that we can somehow alter the masterpiece is obtainable. The reality is we believe that beauty is measured outwardly.

For we are God's masterpiece. He has created us anew in Christ Jesus, so we can do the good things he planned for us long ago.
Ephesians 2:10, NLT

I remember when I first heard this verse. For years, I clung to it. On days when my thoughts led me to the fridge, the drive-through, or down the candy aisle, it helped me recover after I lost control and would choose food over truth. Over and over again, I would use my desire for food over Jesus as a crutch. I would say things like, "It's ok that I am big; I am still God's masterpiece." There is truth in that statement. I truly believe no matter what size I am or you are, God looks at us with heart

By Guarding What You've Been Given

eyes and loves what He created. However, the problem is that I lost many opportunities to make memories and see God work for years because of this mindset.

One of the things that breaks my heart to this day is the amount of time I lost with my kids. I don't ever remember one memory of me playing in the sand with my kids or running and chasing them on the beach. Instead, when I was on the beach, I would stay put in a chair covered up. I wouldn't move out of that chair because of what everyone behind me would see when I got up. They would see my back fat hanging over the back of my bathing suit and the cellulite gathered on my knees and thighs. They would notice the fat flapping in the wind and wouldn't like me because I wasn't pretty. My poor girls got little to NO beach time with me over the last twenty years because of my deep insecurities rooted in a lie. Somehow, my eyes were on myself. I recently read this verse with new eyes, and oh my goodness, friend, I hope it connects in your heart and mind, too, so that you can see yourself differently and experience freedom.

The word masterpiece in other versions is workmanship.

Let's look at this verse again.

> ***For we are His workmanship, created in Christ Jesus for good works, which God prepared beforehand that we should walk in them.***
> Ephesians 2:10, NKJV

When we are focused on the masterpiece, everything becomes about us. But when we focus on the one who created the masterpiece, it becomes about the skill of the one creating. If I walked into the Dollar Tree and grabbed a vase, no one would ooh and ahh over it. They would be more interested in the flowers in the vase. But if I purchased a vase from someone famous, and I knew that a famous person had created the vase, suddenly, no one would focus on the flowers.

Freedom is when you focus on the Creator and not the created. **We are flawed because of our sinful nature, not because of our design.** Guarding your body has to start with how you see it. If you don't see yourself the way God sees you and choose to believe it, your relationships, your ministry, your dreams, and your life will always feel like they are lacking. I didn't even recognize the lack of intimacy I missed out on with my kids for twenty years. But now I know that I can't get that time back.

Now, I see with new eyes.

I remember when my mom got remarried. I was a 9th-grade boy-crazy girl who attended church, but all of my energy went towards getting the boys to notice me and friends to want to be around me. I will never forget the first time my stepdad came into my room and told me to cut off the music playing before I went to sleep. I fussed and probably said some disrespectful things, but ultimately, he won. Every night, I had to go to sleep without music, and for a long time, I hated it. He said I needed to do that for the sole purpose of God speaking to me. He said, "Holly, all you do is go go go and do do do, and you're never still. How do you think God is ever going to talk to you?" Fast forward to now, and I crave the silence. I look forward to being alone with God because it aligns my heart and mind with His truth so that I can live out what He has purposed me to do from the beginning of time. If I don't read the word, I will not believe I am worthy. I will be at war with how the world says I am supposed to look, and that could send me back into a place of bondage and self-hatred.

How you describe your body to others says much about how you feel about yourself. It's true, and whether you want to admit it or not, guarding your body will bring awareness to your words.

Healthy awareness shines the light on the areas where you

By Guarding What You've Been Given

may be dishonoring God with your body, such as your eating habits. Do you run to the fridge when you're hungry, or when you're bored, or emotionally spiraling? Do you rest? Are you exhausted? Could the exhaustion you hang your hat on not actually be from busyness but instead be disobedience in choosing to scroll on TikTok for hours while choosing not to rest? What are you thinking about and dwelling on all the time? Your thoughts can derail you, taking you down a road of comparison and defeat.

We can shift our blame from one thing to the next without ever allowing God to change us from the inside out, and guarding your body means you are protecting all of your body.

Rebekah is my oldest daughter. Everyone thinks she looks just like me, but I think she looks like her dad, except with long, curly hair. I have issues with constant frizz, and the gray hairs keep popping up, but Rebekah seems to always be in a good hair season. She spends money on products to ensure growth, keep frizz away, and hold curls intact. Several years ago, I was trying out a new vacuum cleaner. As Rebekah sat on our kitchen floor, washing the bottom part of our chairs, she stopped and lay across the floor to tell me a story. I playfully knocked the vacuum into her side as she lay there, and we laughed every time I prodded her. Suddenly, the vacuum stuck to her head, sucking up her hair. She began to scream, calling me a psychopath. I tried not to laugh while I tried to calm her down, but nothing worked because she was hysterical. She angrily yelled at me, saying, "If I have to cut my hair, I will never speak to you again!" Thankfully, we are still speaking. Despite my internal panic, I grabbed a screwdriver and took the vacuum apart, unraveling her hair strand by strand until it was free. Rebekah's reaction may have seemed over the top, but it was born from the fact that she cherishes her hair. Her hair gets the most compliments, so why wouldn't she want to protect it, right?

Protect What You Cherish

If we cherish something, we protect it; the enemy knows that.

Our feelings attached to thoughts of defeat can become an instrument for the enemy to use against us, keeping us from seeing God clearly. Our thoughts have the potential to move us forward or keep us stuck. The problem isn't wanting to feel good about ourselves or even have a level of confidence; it's what we do with those thoughts that follow. Think about how many thoughts run through your head each day. The thoughts that seem to carry the most weight aren't the small ones. It's the thoughts that come when we get ignored at the grocery store by someone we thought we were friends with or the thoughts that come after that "great idea" gets shut down. When your friend forgets your birthday, or your spouse forgets your anniversary. What about the thoughts that follow after discovering that your spouse is addicted to porn? Maybe it was hurtful words spoken to or about you by someone you care deeply for. Those kinds of thoughts can send you spiraling out of control. If you aren't careful, you can find yourself in a very dark place, no longer protecting this body God has given you.

Ladies, our purpose on this earth is to bring God glory. If we allow our thoughts to become the compass of our hearts, then any stirring of a God-sized dream in us will suddenly begin to slow down. It is because our fleshly desires seem more attainable, which leads us to try to protect those things more over surrendering the very thoughts that keep us in that place of defeat.

When protecting our bodies, we must steer our thoughts toward peace, NOT chaos.

You will keep him in perfect peace, all who trust in you, all whose thoughts are fixed on you!
Isaiah 26:3

By Guarding What You've Been Given

I used to have a problem with texting and driving. I know that's not something you do (or admit), but sometimes I just need to say one or two things. I now love the talk-text feature or sending a voice memo for convenience or safety purposes. HA!

A few years ago, I was trying to return a text, and my daughter Rachel yelled that I was running off the road. She said, "Mom, you aren't teaching me about not texting and driving." OUCH, right? I steered our car in what could have potentially been a fatal mistake. The yelling, the frustration, and the chaos happened because I took my eyes away from what I was supposed to be doing to what I desired to do.

When our thoughts run towards the truths of God's Word for protection, they can bring about change and not derail us. I could have yelled back, and I am sure I did say something like, "You are not my boss." But I could have let those thoughts give way to thoughts of not being a good mom or questions about why I try in ministry when I can't even lead my own kids. See how toxic thoughts can follow one outburst?

Thoughts are a breeding ground for toxins, allowing them to attack the truths we have swept under the rug of our hearts, letting our desires and emotions take center stage. Satan used the same tactics on Eve in the Garden of Eden, and you, sweet friend, are no different. Where are your thoughts headed, even now, as you read the words on this page? Do your relationships reflect the toxins sitting in the corners of your heart? Does how you view your calling and dreams reflect the truths of who God says you are?

I often create stories in my head based on my surroundings. Some of those stories created in my head began with an irrational thought. I am not talking about those kinds of thoughts. I am talking about the thoughts that follow heartache, insecurities, and fears; the thoughts that derail you from seeing the goodness

Protect What You Cherish

of God and His power. I believe our thought patterns reveal so much about our hearts, and it is shown in how we treat our bodies. As emotions begin to stir in us based on how we feel, we tend to lean in favor of how we can elevate ourselves above any kind of change, discipline, or admission of weakness. These thought patterns chain us to our never-ending insecurities. We then create scenarios and manipulate outcomes because we fear facing the very things God may be calling out of us. I do believe with all my heart that God is a God of unending grace, yet I believe the whispers of His redeeming love are meant to be our call to relinquish the control we desperately crave. That's why we protect the things we cherish with our claws out, just like a mama bear protects her cubs. We believe it's up to us to keep things in line, on course, and perfect. Nothing is perfect except for Jesus. ***But ladies, God is calling all those toxins lingering within your thought life out of you today.*** He wants your thoughts to be fixed on Him so you can experience His perfect peace. Let this verse once again resonate in your heart. Sit with it, meditate on it, and allow your thoughts to align with this truth.

You will keep him in perfect peace, all who trust in you, all whose thoughts are fixed on you!
Isaiah 26:3

Friends, this verse should give you peace. The kind of peace that feels like sitting around a bonfire with s'mores and a good cup of coffee on a crisp fall night kind of peace. It is your toes in the sand while watching those big waves crash into the shore kind of peace. It's the calm within the storm, even when the winds are recklessly blowing, that kind of peace. It is PERFECT peace. How do we get there? How do we tangibly embrace God's Word and apply it to those toxic thoughts? The enemy waits with eagerness to use your past and any other dark moments that bring in defeating thoughts, hoping to get you off course. You see, the darkness lurking and waiting is like a vulture flying around death. If the enemy can get us to let go of our dreams, our marriages, or the desire to be in the presence of God, he can set in motion his plan to steal, kill, and destroy the very things you once set out to protect.

> *Be anxious for nothing, but in everything by prayer and supplication with thanksgiving, let your requests be made known to God. And the peace of God which surpasses all understanding will guard your hearts and minds through Christ Jesus.*
> Philippians 4:6-7, NKJV

This verse is packed full of truth. Let's take a deeper look. I pulled out a few things to help guard your body by protecting your mind.

Be anxious for nothing . . .

I wish it said, "Be anxious when your bill is due, and there is no money." I wish it said, "Be a little anxious when you walk into the doctor's room and have to hear the diagnosis." I wish I could look you in the face and tell you it's okay to be anxious when you hold that rejection letter to the college of your choice. But ladies, this verse is straightforward: **we must be anxious for nothing.** I am sorry that the enemy has tricked you into thinking it's okay to let even the smallest anxious thought in. He lied, and that one anxious thought breeds more anxious thoughts, and before too long, you are believing lie upon lie. Today is your day to no longer believe his lies. God sees you and wants you to know that you should no longer allow worry and anxiety to be a part of your decision-making. I am not talking about the anxiety that comes from chemical imbalances or a medical condition. I am speaking directly to the ones who allow worry and anxious thinking to be the center of every decision, or the lack thereof, be the driving force behind their anxiety. The anxiety from people pleasing or shame stems from the lack of control in an area.

... but in everything by prayer ...

In all decisions. That means who to marry, who to allow to speak into your life, what kind of car to buy, or when to move. God literally means to talk to Him about everything. He wants you to bring all your heartache, dreams, relationships, and decisions to Him so that He can begin the process of calming your fears by changing the way you think. It's inviting Him into the very place you need Him to protect. You and I need Jesus. He already knows every secret, every dream, every hidden agenda, and every motivation that sneaks into the parts of our minds, compelling us to protect those cherished desires that are within us. It's prayer that moves God to a place of making Himself known. He doesn't need us to pray to change things. He wants us to experience Him through prayer to strengthen our faith.

What are you holding on to so tightly that needs to be released through prayer?
(Write it out.)

... supplication with thanksgiving ...

When trying to change our thought life from breeding toxins to allowing life-giving thoughts, we have to shift our focus from all the destructive thoughts to thanksgiving. Offer up all that you are thankful for, including the goodness of who God is, and before too long, the thing or person or dream you are holding onto so tightly in order to protect will become weightless; you have handed it over to the God who handles all things. The God of the Bible that sees all, knows all, and never leaves us through it all. Thanksgiving is medicine to the mind and a sweet aroma to the soul. It's understanding who God is and allowing Him to take the seat of your heart without any strings attached. He won't put up a fight if we reject Him, but He will pull us in through sweet sunsets and landscapes of His creative nature so that we are drawn to thank Him. It sets surrender in motion when we offer up thanksgiving.

By Guarding What You've Been Given

. . . let your requests be made known to God . . .
Let this part sink in a little. What do you need from God right now, in your current season? What request needs to be made known to God? This doesn't mean you are bringing things to God's attention as if He doesn't know; instead, it's getting to a place of admitting you need Him. Making our request known is our way of surrendering control, including the thoughts that come with whatever you think you desperately need. Thoughts that come out of our prayer requests can often turn into a bargaining session with God. We ask God to do something big and promise to do something in return. God doesn't work that way. He just wants your heart, and attached to our hearts are our thoughts.

This is my favorite part of the verse.

. . . and the <u>peace of God</u> which surpasses all understanding <u>will guard your hearts and minds</u> through Christ Jesus.

All those things listed above lead us to the peace of God while guarding our hearts and minds. It's praying from a place of "I can't," "I give up," "I am scared," and so on that disarms the enemy's attack against you. The truths we embrace through His word begin to stand at attention, waiting for anything that looks nothing like the truth to fight back, and His Word never loses. His power never grows dull, and the enemy never stands a chance.

My youngest daughter, Rachel, was into makeup for a few years. She can still apply it better than anyone I know. Her ability to take color and use techniques to transform someone's face is mind-blowing. She would use every bit of her birthday, Christmas, or allowance money to buy a $80 palette. She would watch YouTube and read blogs to stay on top of what was going on in the makeup world. What I have learned about guarding my thoughts is much like how Rachel approached

Protect What You Cherish

her make-up. She would ensure her face was clean and use extra products like primer and setting spray to create the perfect workspace for her makeup. Her makeup always stays perfectly in place.

God has given us minds to dream, create, reflect, and remember His Word. We can work things out and process the hard stuff. He doesn't want us to dwell in places of regret but, instead, allow His Truth to be the foundation on which everything is built so it keeps us planted firmly in Him. You are not meant to stay in the darkness of who the enemy tells you are, but the darkness is where the thoughts of not measuring up will grow if we don't keep our minds fixed on Him.

Before jumping into the next chapter, please pause and reflect on what you have just read. In the space below, write out the toxins you have harbored within your mind or ways you haven't protected your body. This isn't for you to feel shame or guilt; it is to bring it to the light so the enemy can no longer taunt you with it. It's time for you to be entirely free.

Your heart and mind reflect how you feel about your body. Think about how when those things are aligned with God's word, they have the power to change everything. We have much to cover in the following chapters, so don't stop now. A renewed mind is a freed mind.

CHAPTER 3

Blessed is the man
who walks not in the counsel of the wicked,
nor stands in the way of sinners,
nor sits in the seat of scoffers;
2 but his delight is in the law of the Lord,
and on his law he meditates day and night.
Psalm 1:1-2 ESV

Guard Your Calling

I have always loved telling stories. I am a visual learner, so creating images in my mind helps me bring the most creative and imaginative stories to life. When my girls were younger, I told them about a fairy named Hillary who lived in an enchanted garden. Every night before bed, my girls would say, "Mommy, please, just one more story about Hillary." The stories were, of course, made up of fake characters and scenery, yet the lessons seemed to get the point across at bedtime. I would let go of the dishes, laundry, and other household chores just so I could take them to this enchanted forest in their little minds and teach them a lesson or two.

Usually, the story contained some sort of cliffhanger moment where Hillary (the fairy) is supposed to follow through with something that is attached to obedience. When she didn't, she always ended up in trouble and on the run from Larry the troll.

I wish I could say I obeyed the voice of God every single time I knew He was calling me to do, say, or go places. But if I am honest, there have been days I have disobeyed. I masked it with "doing things for God" or what I like to call the "ministry hustle." I chased people to move me forward in what God had called me. I chased approval, appearance, and assignments over the appointing and commissioning. Looking back, it took a lot of tears, repentance, and challenging conversations with God to understand I was chasing a calling over the One who had called me.

In this chapter, I want to talk about what it looks like to guard our giftings so it helps us live out the callings in our lives. If we are going to guard our callings, our first step is to surrender it. Surrender is a word you often hear in church settings, yet it seems complicated to do tangibly. I have walked down front in the church a time or two with my hands open and sobbing, as if I was holding the very thing I needed to surrender, and yet got up, walked out the doors, and felt the same. I have felt the pain of hearing the word no and what seemed as if I was being looked over more times than I can count. But it wasn't until I was tired and worn out emotionally, spiritually, and physically that things shifted. I had to get to the end of me to see God's protection, provision, and perfect way.

I love the story in the Bible about a man who is someone I would call a hero. Y'all it even talks about poop in the Bible (but that's not the point of the story). His story is beautiful, and it's filled with adventure, risk, obedience, victory, and peace. God used a man to kill a corrupt king, an act which brought peace. I believe God wants to use your uniqueness, which you may call weaknesses, to change your homes, marriages, community, churches, and schools, all for His glory.

My husband calls him "Ehud, the left-handed dude."

Grab your Bible, because I want you to mark and read a little as we go through this together. Judges 3:7 is where we will begin.

In Judges 3, Ehud was raised for one purpose; he was a part

of delivering peace into the hands of the Israelites. It started with the disobedience of the Israelites (yet again).

And the people of Israel did what was evil in the sight of the Lord. They forgot the Lord their God and served the Baals and the Asheroth.
Judges 3:7, ESV

Ehud came on the scene, and everything changed.

Then the people of Israel cried out to the LORD, and the LORD raised up for them a deliverer, Ehud, the son of Gera, the Benjaminite, a left-handed man. The people of Israel sent tribute by him to Eglon the king of Moab.
Judges 3:15, ESV

One of the things I love about Ehud is he responded to the call with instant obedience. He didn't second-guess it or sit in it; he didn't ask people if he should or shouldn't do it. The Bible doesn't record his hesitancy. Instead, Ehud boldly and confidently walked into the king's quarters, ready to do what needed to happen.

18 And when Ehud had finished presenting the tribute, he sent away the people who carried the tribute. 19 But he himself turned back at the idols near Gilgal and said, "I have a secret message for you, O king." And he commanded, "Silence." And all his attendants went out from his presence. 20 And Ehud came to him as he was sitting alone in his cool roof chamber. And Ehud said, "I have a message from God for you." And he arose from his seat. 21 And Ehud reached with his left hand, took the sword from his right thigh, and thrust it into his belly. 22 And the hilt also went in after the blade, and the fat closed over the blade, for he did not pull the sword out of his belly; and the dung came out. 23 Then Ehud went out into the porch[b]

and closed the doors of the roof chamber behind him and locked them.
Judges 3:18-23, ESV

How many times have you known you were called to do something, but instead, you held back or said, "I will pray about it?" Have you ever thought that if God has the power to give you a specific purpose to carry out, He also won't let anyone stop it? We allow so much of our doubts and unbelief to distract and derail us from walking in obedience.

Our callings are just that—our callings. God may use someone in your life to fan that flame, or even become a bridge, but it comes down to trusting God while responding without hesitation. Obedience is not choosing to stand still; instead, it requires an intentional movement towards Jesus.

Be still and know that I am God.
Psalms 46:10 NIV

We have all quoted this scripture or purchased a printed t-shirt or household item with the verse.

The words "be still" translated in the NASB version is a game changer.

Stop striving and know that I am God; I will be exalted among the nations,
I will be exalted on the earth.
Psalm 46:10, NASB

It is an active command. It's a call for you and me to stop striving. To "stop" means it's an intentional movement on our part to get our effort and energy off of anything other than God. It is exhausting our earthly strength while learning to lean wholly on the power and strength of God. The problem comes when we allow our identity to no longer be in Christ but, instead, in what we do.

In our minds, we build expectations of everything we don't have or everything that's wrong with our current season. We begin to doubt God, and then distance ourselves from the very thing He has called us to do. If the enemy can get you to doubt one thing, he knows getting you to doubt two things will be a piece of cake. The truth about who we think we are dictates our every step and how we walk in the dreams we desire to come true. We talk about our passions, think about them, and read about related things but never move beyond the thought.

In Acts, Paul is working as a tentmaker (tent maker) and sharing the gospel. His drive to move the kingdom forward blows me away. Verses 9-11 in chapter 18 remind me of two beautiful truths I want to share with you:

One night the Lord spoke to Paul in a vision 'Do not be afraid; keep on speaking do not be silent. For I am with you and no one is going to attack and harm you, because I have many people in this city.' So Paul stayed in Corinth for a year and a half, teaching them the word of God.

It says, "Keep on speaking." This, to me, must have come at a time when Paul was working a long week, tired, and living in a house with a family he didn't know very well. Yet, on the weekends, he gave all he had trying to win people to Jesus. Was he discouraged? Maybe ready to give up? How often have you been in this spot, where you needed a little extra nudge from God to keep going?

Secondly, it says he stayed for a year and a half longer, teaching them the Word of God. That's a lot of days. I look at seasons where, just two weeks into something, I'm exhausted and ready to throw in the towel, all in the name of Jesus. What I am realizing is the length of a season literally has nothing to do with my obedience but everything to do with my disobedience. When we serve God out of duty, any length will quickly turn to bitterness and frustration, and in the end, we can miss the presence of God. When we choose to serve out of our love for Him, above all else, peace and freedom flow. We see Him clearly and are satisfied, so we love from a place of wholeness, not hopelessness.

Ministry can feel like a constant roller coaster. If your identity and value are based on the highs, then when the lows come, you feel thrown off course or defeated.

I always laugh at kids when they want to ride a roller coaster; they cry through the entire ride, yet they are ready to endure it again hours later. I believe it's because they know what to expect the second time. There is so much truth in that. We have been called and chosen to share the gospel daily, and yet, we also know the enemy's one job is to derail us over and over and over again. It is when we ask ourselves, **What am I passionate about? Is it more than God? Am I being obedient with my gifts?**

Hard questions, like those above, lead us to more profound holiness, because if we are followers of Jesus, we have to know that it's in those moments of honest reflection we see the places we continue to walk in disobedience. When we repent, God removes the unnecessary space the enemy wants to keep between us and God.

Let's look back at Judges 3:12-15:

> *12 And the people of Israel again did what was evil in the sight of the Lord, and the Lord strengthened Eglon the king of Moab against Israel, because they had done what was evil in the sight of the Lord. 13 He gathered to himself the Ammonites and the Amalekites, and went and defeated*

By Guarding What You've Been Given

Israel. And they took possession of the city of palms. 14 And the people of Israel served Eglon the king of Moab eighteen years. 15 Then the people of Israel cried out to the Lord, and the Lord raised up for them a deliverer, Ehud, the son of Gera, the Benjaminite, a left-handed man. The people of Israel sent tribute by him to Eglon the king of Moab.

It doesn't say Ehud was passionate about people. It doesn't say he is a great singer or writer. It only gives me who his dad is and that he is left-handed. The very thing that looked like a weakness was the very thing God used to slay the king and bring peace. I don't want to skip over one line in verse 15 packed with power: "The Lord raised up for them a deliverer, Ehud."

It was God who created Him to be left-handed, in a generation of evil, and to be the deliverer.

Right now, where you are, God has also placed you to carry out His name. Don't let doubt or insecurities cause you to second-guess yourself or, even more, God's hand in your purpose. It is often in the midst of second-guessing our abilities that God reveals His power so we can carry out what we were so hesitant even to begin.

I remember walking off stage at an event where I was speaking and wanting to binge eat so badly; it was like my emotions and desires were fighting within my soul. I drove to a store before returning to the hotel and bought chips, cookies, and candy. I remember almost inhaling it; it's like I couldn't eat it fast enough. I had just stood on stage declaring freedom, but at that exact moment, my weakness was the voice I listened to. I thought, somehow, those treats would lead me to a place of satisfaction, but it didn't; it only made me feel like a fraud. Looking back, I can see things differently now. I went into that speaking engagement barely on time, hungry, and trying to impress those in the audience. After that message, people responded to God's word, and many were on their knees. Was it my fear of looking "too fat" on stage? Was it my fear that no one would get what I was trying to say? No, God's Word and the Holy Spirit stirred and changed the atmosphere that night. My disobedience led me to repentance later, because I realized that instead of celebrating and worshiping God, I worshiped and bowed to the very thing that had landed me to that place of ever declaring Freedom in the first place. We can't use insecurities to fight our fleshly desires. It is like fighting with a sword of lies, which gets you nowhere. However, something shifts when we surrender the lies by embracing the truth of God's Word. Although we feel weak, we can stand stronger because we fight from a place where God is in complete control, and we are okay with whatever He calls us to because we know He will see us through.

In Judges 3, Ehud straps a sword to his left leg because he is left-handed, which is his advantage. Going through the security, they checked the other side, thinking he was unarmed and right-handed. I bet his heart was pounding going through those armed security guys. The adrenaline was pumping, heart pounding, and at any moment, they could have checked the other leg, and he would have been exposed. BUT GOD, right? When our obedience collides with God's power and plan, **NOTHING can stop a move of God.** Those men were not going to stop Ehud's assignment because those men were not in charge.

Just like your assignment here on earth. Your parents, your siblings, your friends, your bosses, or your enemies do not have the power to stop your assignment from being carried out, but the enemy will use them to distract you. Whether it's wanting to gain approval or listening to the cons of why you shouldn't, those things distract you from carrying out God's assignment, but they will not stop God. He will just use someone else.

By Guarding What You've Been Given

How can we guard our callings?

The first step is to stop trying to carry out your callings in your own strength. You cannot do it. You cannot do it. You cannot do it. I don't know how much clearer I can be. It will never be because of you. Instead, it will be because God has ordained, gifted, opened doors, and allowed it to happen, and the sooner we believe that the easier it is to walk confidently in what He has called us to do. It also frees you up from manipulating the outcome. You can work hard and carry a lot, yet never do what God has called you specifically to do. We often allow our emotions to get tangled up with our call to follow through with obedience, leading us in the opposite direction of carrying out what we were called to do in the first place. Let me explain.

Let's say God has called you to start a Bible study. You are passionate about people knowing God's Word, and you are excited to gain a deeper community centered on the Word. But one morning, you get a text saying, **Who will teach the Bible study? I mean, do you know enough to teach?** That statement can make you second guess something God has called you to do. You let it fizzle out before you even meet once simply because of fear. The truth is we can't do anything outside of God's power. It is His spirit in us that helps us do what He has called and equipped us to do. There are a lot of voices competing for our attention, affection, and ears. Whether it be social media or our friends, everyone seems to have an opinion of how things should play out or what you should be doing. To guard your calling, you have to silence the views and choose to lean into God's word and truth. Will people confirm things? Sometimes, but how can things be confirmed if you aren't praying about it? Step back and ask yourself: Am I seeking God while trying to do what I am called to do in this season? Or am I leaning on myself or others to get me through?

For it is [not your strength, but it is] God who is effectively at work in you, both to will and to work [that is, strengthening, energizing, and creating in you the longing and the ability to fulfill your purpose] for His good pleasure.
Philippians 2:13, AMP

If you try to do it with your own strength, you will burn out, quit trying, and believe the lies the enemy is telling you about yourself and what God has called you to be passionate about.

Sweet friend, don't stop. Take your next step in the pathway of where Jesus is. If He isn't in it, don't pursue it.

Secondly, if you want to guard your calling, you have to recognize the risk that comes with obedience. I have seen so many people walk away from what seemed like the most challenging season of their lives, from losing friendships with people they love to having doors shut to loss that led to profound grief. The grief seemed like too much, so they chose to go back, simply because the feeling of losing comfort or a friendship was too much for them to bear.

Grief is something I will never fully understand, but I do know I can't find anywhere in the Bible where comfort was an option to remain in when there was a call to obedience. From the miracles performed by Jesus to the disciples leaving everything to follow Him, every encounter came with loss of comfort. It comes down to a choice. Will I choose to remain in disobedience simply because of fear? Or, will I take a bold step of obedience even if it requires me to be highly uncomfortable? Self-reflection is an excellent way to survey the areas of your life to see if you are pursuing comfort or walking in bold obedience. If your days run together and look the same without risk, then you may be sitting in comfort. Throughout scripture, there is a recurring theme of people choosing hard, and most of the time, it was life-threatening: the story

By Guarding What You've Been Given

of Abraham and Issac to Esther entering the King's Courts to Daniel in the lion's den to Ehud the left-handed dude sneaking past the guards. They all had a choice to make, knowing that death could be an option, and yet, they chose to be obedient.

I will never forget when Rachel was in her elementary talent show. She chose to dance to a Toby Mac song. She was confident and didn't care about anything other than getting up there and dancing her heart out. Everyone was clapping and cheering her on, and she soaked it up. However, fast forward years later to standing in a dance class where someone said some harsh things to her. From that point on, she no longer chose to dance. She was wounded to the point of quitting, and it crushed my heart. I didn't care about her dancing but how that moment would shape how she saw herself and responded to hard things in the future. That year, she stuck it out and stayed until the end of the year, and she danced beautifully at her recital but never walked into another dance studio after that. The truth is, some moments will knock the breath out of you. There will always be people who will try and derail you from following Jesus wholeheartedly. There will be people, even in ministry, who will say mean things to you. Those people will do their best to convince you that you aren't the person for the job or you can't do something. They will remind you of your past and try to block you by feeding your insecurities and withholding validation.

BUT, God will use those things for good because that is who God is. I now see Rachel preparing to teach again in her life group. She went to Africa with an organization where she knew no one. She hosts our yearly girls' event and is learning to push through hard seasons. Words that were meant to destroy her actually propelled her. It wasn't anything she did but everything God was doing through her. Does she still struggle? Yes, but she is fighting by choosing not to give in to the voices of doubt inside her own head.

When we surrender our callings, understand that they are not about ourselves, and choose to do them regardless of how we feel, it postures our hearts to no longer desire an outcome of our own doing but, instead, trust God has the perfect plan. If we are using our gifts without worry, could you imagine the number of things we could see in our lifetime? Ehud inspires me so much because he did what he was raised to do, and eighty years of peace followed.

Imagine if you could bring peace to someone simply by obeying God's voice and doing what He has gifted and called you to do.

If you work in retail and you have the opportunity to encourage people, do it with your whole heart.

If you are working at a drive-in window, you can serve people well.

If you are sitting at a desk in a high-rise building, do it with your whole heart.

But remember, within your job, there are assignments to point people to Jesus. That person sitting beside you or one staff member who seems to always be on the same shift as you is never by mistake. God is up to something, bringing you in to be a part of it.

Take a moment and write down all the places you go and who is currently surrounding you in those places (school, work, church, gym, etc.). Then, ask God to open your eyes to see things differently.

God will never leave you.

I will never forget the first time I felt this major tug on my heart to start a girls' ministry. I was deep into my struggle with body image issues along with food addiction. I was serving in our student ministry as a volunteer. We were at a concert/conference in Charlotte, and Natalie Grant was on stage. It was the first time I had ever seen or heard her, and y'all, as she shared her personal struggles and began to sing, I remember crying so hard that the students asked if I was okay. The truth was, I wasn't OK, but it was in the best way. Natalie's obedience unlocked freedom in me that day, but also, that was the moment I felt the stirring for girls' ministry. A passion was born in me from that point forward; that day and now, twenty-one years later, my heart is for girls and women to know Jesus and to walk fully in freedom. Do I wish I could sing like Natalie? Ummm, who doesn't? HA! However, I know my gift is encouraging girls to pursue Jesus wholeheartedly while speaking life and freedom into them. I want every girl to know their worth and freedom in Christ.

We must be careful in guarding our callings because comparison will fight ugly, create space, cause division, and keep us from experiencing freedom. We allow comparison to enslave us to the opinions of others and to the expectations we put on ourselves. The truth is you will only measure up to the world's standards if the measuring stick moves.

I would start by asking myself things like:

What am I good at doing?
What keeps me up at night?
What am I passionate about?
Who's in front of me right now?

Don't allow the enemy to tell you your calling can only be fulfilled if you are on a stage, have the next best-selling book, or are the best in your school or career. THAT IS NOT TRUE. When you allow your heart to align with God's Word, you begin to see things differently. Guarding our calling doesn't mean you are inactive; it means you love, serve, and do what is in front of you wholeheartedly. I have watched many doors open and shut for me over the years, and looking back, I can clearly see God was stirring something new in me while also protecting me. Our wants don't always align with the truth, and because God is a God that transforms us from the inside out, He often begins with transforming our desires. Sweet friend, if God isn't in the equation, it is NOT for you. If God shuts the door, don't reopen it because His ways are perfect. If you aren't meant to walk through that door, don't.

It's time to understand and embrace that you genuinely do have a purpose in this world. You have something to offer to the people in your corner of the world. You have something to offer the people who are hurting and lost, and your obedience is your next step in the journey. Take a few moments to write out a prayer of surrender. Ask God to fan the flame in you for what He has called you and gifted you to do. I believe if you start serving those in front of you, God will continue to light up the path where you are to step next. Whether on a stage, in a village in another country, or leading a small group, you will know it's your next step because God will put a desire in your heart to do it.

Before I finish this chapter, I want to remind you that the attacks of the enemy will never outweigh the power of the Creator who called you. The older I get, the more I see the enemy's schemes, and yet the bolder I get in standing firm in Jesus, which is not a skill or passion He has given me. I see God's Word as a guide to steward what He has made me passionate about, which has changed me. Every time I get on social media, I see people attacking other people's political parties, the church, and how people do things. Sometimes, people just want to complain or post their opinions because they are disobedient and need to feel better about it. However, I also believe there will always be things and people who come against the work of the Lord. If you are there, I want to encourage you to stand firm, keep

By Guarding What You've Been Given

going, and do what God has set before you. Nothing can stop what God intends to use through you but YOU.

Psalm 91 has become a new anthem for me, and I hope it encourages you, too.

> *Whoever dwells in the shelter of the Most High*
> *will rest in the shadow of the Almighty. I will say of the*
> *Lord, "He is my refuge and my fortress, my God, in whom I*
> *trust." Surely he will save you*
> *from the fowler's snare*
> *and from the deadly pestilence.*
> *He will cover you with his feathers,*
> *and under his wings you will find refuge;*
> *his faithfulness will be your shield and rampart*
> Psalm 91:1-4 NIV

He will cover you with His feathers. Those words have been like ointment to my soul in seasons of doubting or fighting against the words of those who tried to knock me out of what God has called me to. God alone is our refuge, and He alone is all I need (and you need) to finish well and accomplish mighty things in His name for His glory. Imagine me standing beside you, cheering as loudly as possible for you. I want you to step into freedom while doing what you love and what is hard and what is holy. It won't be easy, but that's OK, because you've been equipped.

Protect What You Cherish

By Guarding What You've Been Given

CHAPTER 4

Bears that successfully meet the caloric minimum
can survive on fat stores for their entire hibernation period.[7]

Guard Your Time

Growing up, my family was never on time for anything. If it was going to school, we made it in the door right before the bell was about to ring or was ringing. If it was clogging class, we were notorious for being at least fifteen to thirty minutes late to practice, and sometimes, we were even putting on our clogging shoes and makeup for competitions as we pulled into the parking lot. But for church, my mom would do whatever it took to get us as close to on time as possible.

Sometimes, we got in just before worship ended and before the preacher started to preach, but we made it. My mom was a single mom who ensured we were where we needed to be and had what we needed. One of the things I am grateful for today is how she guarded my time. She made me attend church on Sunday mornings, Sunday nights, and every Wednesday. It was a way of life for us, whether I wanted to go or not, but nothing got in the way of us going to church. There were many Sundays that, if we couldn't be there, we had our preacher on the radio and listened as we drove. She guarded our time by ensuring we invested in our souls week in and week out. She prioritized her time in the Word, and I watched her, and I cherish that.

This chapter examines the concept of time and the importance of guarding it. We must understand three things:

Time is a gift.
Time isn't an excuse for laziness.
Time tells the story of where our hearts are.

Let's return to God's Word to see what God says about time.

In Ecclesiastes, it says this,

For everything there is a season, and a time for every matter under heaven.
Ecclesiastes 3:1

Isn't it funny how we complain most days about not having enough time? We don't have enough time to clean, return calls or texts, do what we want to do or the things we don't want to, and yet, we somehow find the time to do things like binge-watch an entire Netflix series or scroll for endless hours on social media. I don't always believe it's not about having enough time; we don't choose to guard our time.

We have to remember that:

Time is a gift.

Life has a beginning and an ending, and God gives us the moments in between. For some people, that time is cut short by tragedy and death, and though I will never understand it, I know our lives have a time stamp on them. If you are here reading this, you still have a purpose, and God wants to use you today.

Let's look back at Ehud for a moment.

Ehud was raised at the perfect time in history. His obedience brought peace to the Israelites, but it was all in God's perfect timing. Again, let me say this: if you are reading this book in

By Guarding What You've Been Given

3043, know you were placed in this historical period for a purpose. Just like Ehud, you are a gift and here because God's ways are perfect, and His timing is always perfect. But could you imagine if Ehud would have begun to doubt or wallow in fear or insecurities? I wouldn't be talking about how he had responded immediately, that's for sure.

Ehud's story gives me the bold courage to respond to the assignments laid out before me daily.

The number of times I have said, "I'm sorry I'm late," usually has everything to do with my lack of time management and nothing to do with time stealing something from me. From waking up too late because I chose to stay up too late to complain about my kids dragging me to get ready when I didn't have their clothes cleaned or prepared. All of those things fall under lack of time management.

I believe God has gifted us with time to enjoy life, people, and do the things we love, but also, chasing daylight for the purpose of leading people to Jesus has to be on the agenda on other days than Sunday or the weeks you have marked aside for mission trips or summer camp. We tend to make our time about furthering ourselves rather than furthering the kingdom. The reality is when we think the time we sleep, the time we have on vacation, the time we are at work or sports is our time, we already have a distorted view, because we have made our lives about us. Think about this. When was the last time you woke up, grabbed your cup of coffee, and asked God to show you, direct you, and open your eyes to His assignments for the day? Y'all, could you imagine how differently our day to day would look? If you have been doing the same things for weeks, months, and years, I would say you cannot be exercising your time for the kingdom fully. If we live as if time is a gift, there is no way we would allow apathy and laziness to creep up and guide our days.

Protect What You Cherish

Time isn't something you can borrow or get back; knowing this is why it's essential to guard the time we have been given here on earth.

Guarding your time may look like saying no to that thing that always has you away from being in church.

Guarding your time may look like putting your phone away at night so you can rest and be fully alert and ready for the following day.

Guarding your time may mean stepping away from a hobby so that you are ready for where God may send you or who He may need you to pour into.

Guarding your time may mean waking up with the mindset that the day ahead of you isn't for you to accomplish a task but to walk with your heart postured towards the Lord so you can be aware of spontaneous God moments.

Guarding your time may mean setting an alarm every hour to pray for someone in your life or an area where you are desperate for God to move.

Guarding your time may require that you no longer choose laziness and apathy.

Once we understand that time is a beautiful gift from God, we begin to see things differently.

Several years ago, I was walking out of my friend's house, and I turned my ankle and knew instantly it was cracked. The hospital confirmed it was indeed fractured. It was my driving foot, and for ten weeks, I couldn't drive. I was stuck in a chair, in my home, for most of the day, and what started as a terrible few days and weeks turned into one of the most special times in my life. I will never forget the moment I shifted my perspective. I was so sick of watching TV and sulking about how it stunk that I was stuck. I was staring out the window, and I saw a little bird begin to build a nest. I watched this little bird fly in and out of that nest for hours. It spent most of its daylight gathering.

As I sat there, I remember feeling so helpless, but I also grabbed a pen and a piece of paper and started diving into God's word. He taught me so much during those few weeks that followed. I learned what it meant to rest, to stop striving, and to gather, even in the seasons of no movement. Suddenly, that time looked like a gift, and now, I will always cherish the quiet, bird-watching, soul-nurturing season. The passages God led me to sustained me and carried me in the coming seasons. It would have been easier for me to watch more movies and complain about all that I couldn't do. It was in the gathering that God used that time to prepare me for the coming season.

Then I considered all that my hands had done and the toil I had expended in doing it, and behold, all was vanity and a striving after wind, and there was nothing to be gained under the sun.
Ecclesiastes 2:11

This verse gets me every single time I read it. I have wasted so much time striving in my lifetime, and I am in my forties (see how I avoided my age, HA!). I have so many regrets, conversations I wish I could undo, and actions that led to years of shame and heartache I wish I could undo. So many insecurities that kept me from moving forward while striving for the constant approval of others. I let too much time be filled with ME and not God. If you are in that place now, please know that regret gets you nowhere, and shame isn't from God. Let it go and move on because there is too much kingdom work to be done.

Sometimes, when I look at Ehud's story, I wonder if there were days when he second-guessed his purpose. When all the kids were playing, did his left-handedness keep him from playing with his friends? Did what seemed like his being different ever make him wonder why God made him that way? Did he ever question why God chose him? This leads me to my second point about time.

Time isn't an excuse for laziness.

Let me explain before you get frustrated with me and close this book. I am not talking about cozying up on your couch with a fuzzy blanket and a good book to read on a Saturday evening. Nor am I talking about binge-watching your favorite show on a Tuesday. I am talking about choosing laziness when it comes to growing the kingdom and your heart. Laziness is dictionary-defined as "unwilling to work or use energy."[8]

OUCH.

Unwilling to grow the kingdom or put any energy into it sounds much harsher than saying I am lazy. To me, this is a wake-up call for this generation and future generations to understand that what we invest our time and energy into can't be more important than growing the kingdom of God.

Ephesians 4 puts it this way,

> *Look carefully then. how you walk, not as unwise but as wise, making the best use of the time, because the days are evil. Therefore do not be foolish, but understand what the will of the Lord is.*
> Ephesians 5:15-17, ESV

Let's break this down.

Look carefully.

By Guarding What You've Been Given

To be so intentional with every step is participation on my part when trying to utilize my gift wisely. One misstep can cause you to step in a dangerous direction of apathy, laziness, or even disobedience. Let me give you a tangible example of what it means to "look carefully" in the light of my mission trips to Honduras.

In the villages of Honduras, you can always tell who is from Honduras and who is not. The ones that are from that village walk with purpose down the mountain, and the ones who are not watch every step they take. They look for wild dogs, bugs, snakes, and really anything else that may be harmful. It is almost comical to watch, but it reminds me of this verse because we sometimes get so comfortable with a path well traveled we tend to no longer look for potential threats to our walk. In order to guard the time you have been given, it is imperative to guard each step you take. This passage goes on to say in verse 16, "Not as unwise but as wise, making the best use of time, because the days are evil." That sounds almost harsh, but it's true. Everywhere you take a step is an opportunity to choose something over following Jesus.

Porn is one click away, making a wrong turn in your marriage is one decision away, choosing to have sex with your boyfriend is one decision away, and choosing to go back to your old lifestyle is one decision away.

In one moment, your whole life could change. Let that sit for a moment.

The last part of verse 17 says, "but understand what the will of the Lord is." Friend, YOU ARE HIS WILL. You were chosen to do His work at this time, and every moment and choice you make matters.

Now, let's get back to the lazy part. If we know being lazy spiritually is an action on our part, shouldn't that change how we spend time in God's Word, going to church, and living out the gospel daily? Notice I said we ***should*** change the way we look. Most days, we believe the time we have been given is ours to decide how we will live.

I recently bought a notebook that has sections on it to help my undiagnosed ADHD brain. The first section is "What needs to get done today," which is my "I better get this done or else" list. It is my return a text, email, or phone call reminder, or my don't forget to pick up Richard's medicine reminder. There is another section that says, "Things I want to get done," and those are the things like sending a card in the mail, scheduling a coffee date with the people I mentor or friends, or making sure I have cleared my schedule so that I can go to the movies on opening night. It's the things that fill my heart's desire. None of those are bad; in fact, many of those things are often ministry-related, but if I am not careful, those things can become what my heart desires more than Jesus. When I allow my time to be stolen by things like striving or filling my schedule with things without ever going to Jesus first, seeking the heart of God can quickly look more like a chore than a delight. Friend, striving, whether it be for more things, more success, more self-preservation, or more self-elation, will always lead you into a place of burnout or defeat because the time was spent on building self.

Take a moment and write out a typical day in your life:
Does your day start with Jesus?
Does your schedule allow you to reach out to others or allow others to reach in?
Does your schedule have room for any God-ordained moments that move the gospel from your heart to the lives of others?

I don't want you to think this is a measuring stick of your performance; I just want you to have a clear picture of where your time is being spent.

God isn't mad at you; He simply wants you.

By Guarding What You've Been Given

In Judges 3, one of my favorite parts of the story of Ehud is this verse:

So Moab was subdued that day under the hand of Israel. T
And the land had rest for eighty years.
Judges 3:30, (ESV)

Because Ehud responded with quick obedience, it must have meant he had his ears bent toward the voice of God and his feet ready to move on behalf of Him. He didn't have his schedule so full that He couldn't do the will of the father, and because of that, eighty years of peace came. EIGHTY YEARS. I can't wrap my mind around that, but goodness, don't we need it in our lives and our country? I have been so weighed down in seasons where I allowed the weight to keep me from walking in obedience. Things like anxiety or fear of the unknown have almost stopped me in my tracks from moving forward, and because of that, my peace was disrupted. When I think about how heavy our emotions can take a toll on us, I am reminded of my sweet daughter.

Rachel is my youngest daughter, and she is someone who feels emotions so deeply. She wants others to cut through the small talk, and she recognizes "shallow" from a mile away. She definitely has the gift of discernment, but she's also hyper-aware of people who are not genuine. It takes a lot for her to trust you and even more to let you in. She was hurt deeply a few years ago, and because of that, she closed herself off to a deeper community for a season, and it was so hard to watch her. She struggles with anxiety, depression, and OCD, and there are days she gets out of bed already feeling emotionally beat up and defeated before saying one word. I spend a lot of my time praying for peace over her mind, and yet, I often try to fill those valley moments with things to do simply because I hate her being in that place. But over the last few months, I have found myself shifting my prayers from asking God to heal her mind to also asking Him to do what He needs to bring peace to her mind and full satisfaction to her soul. That is hard for a mama to let go, but I can't do what God can. I can take her to Disney or buy her things, but that doesn't last. I do know that when I pray, it removes me from the equation. Because of those prayers, I have seen her walk through one of the darkest seasons to date. She was having suicidal thoughts to the point someone called us to let us know their concerns. I remember sitting in the living room with Richard. It was quiet, and he sat on one couch, crying and praying. I sat on the other couch, crying and praying for a breakthrough to happen.

Y'ALL, GOD DID IT. He reached into her mind, and He showed her people she needed to forgive, things to lay down, and things she needed to work on. Her friendships have begun to change. She is leading and talking differently, and something is shifting. Is it Healing? Gosh, I hope so, but I also know God's healing and TIMING can look a lot different from our expectations. If it wasn't for that super dark valley, Rachel might have never called the ones who had hurt her the most. She is now working through some new issues; I can honestly say it all began in that valley.

Friends, whether you are struggling with depression, or anxiety, or desperate for God to move in your life, don't stop praying. Don't stop asking God to move; just know His timeline is way better than yours.

> *"For my thoughts are not your thoughts, neither are your ways my ways," declares the Lord.*
> *9 "As the heavens are higher than the earth, so are my ways higher than your ways*
> *and my thoughts than your thoughts."*
> Isaiah 55:8-9 ESV

His way is so much better—it truly is. We want instant healing and all the moments and memories that make us happy. But I

By Guarding What You've Been Given

have watched people closest to me, and even my own junk, take me closer to Jesus in the valley and seasons that seemed forever long, and I wouldn't go back and change a thing.

Is there anything from your past you regret? Gosh, I can think of many things I did as a kid, and for sure, there were some really dumb decisions I made as a teenager. I would love to get that time back. I can also think of many conversations I have replayed over and over in my mind. And though I can think about it all day, the reality is I can't go back in time and do it over or undo what has been done. Words that were spoken that were meant to sting were said, and I can't unsay them. We find ourselves in regret simply because we let a decision dictate whether we feel satisfied or not. The opposite of regret is satisfaction. Guarding your time means you realize that time is something we can't get back. Therefore, with every moment we have here on this earth, we treat it as both special and intentional, knowing that our decisions have a lasting impact.

Recently, I was at the doctor's office with Richard. He was having hand surgery on two fingers. They call it "trigger finger," and it has been bothering him for so long. But after his heart attack, the insurance deductible had been met, so we were racing against the clock to take care of things that he had allowed to linger. Some things were just inconveniences, and we had to wait a little while because medical bills pile up quickly. We were so thankful that there was no deductible and that he is seeing relief in many areas, but it's also sad because a lot of time has passed, and even more damage has been done in the process. Sweet friend, I know that time is something we can't get back, but we can make the most of our time here on Earth. Maybe you must put down this book, pick up your phone, and finally forgive that person who hurt you. Perhaps today, you will decide that social media will no longer steal your joy and keep you in a constant place of striving and comparison. Maybe today, you decide it's finally time to take that bold step of obedience you know God has been calling you to. One of the things I have noticed since Richard's heart attack happened is that family time is sweeter. I enjoy it, but I also crave it. I believe the moment I realized that my time with Richard could have been cut short was the moment I wanted every moment moving forward with him. I don't think time should handcuff us, nor should time be the driver of our chaos. We have the power to say no, and when you cherish your time, you begin to see what truly matters and what actually doesn't need your attention.

I love learning about bears. One of the most fascinating things I learned recently was from an article I read: "Bears are among the most intelligent land animals in North America. They have the largest and most complex brains compared to other land mammals their size, and they rely on this brain for a number of behaviors. For example, grizzly bears can remember hotspots for food even after ten years."[9]

God designed us to soak up every moment by giving us our senses. God perfectly designed you and me so we could step into our generation at the moment God intended. Our time here is important, and it's intentional. I could ask someone where they were on the day 9-11, and they could give me details of their day. Or I can ask someone where they were when they got that call of heartache, and they can provide me details down to what they were wearing. I am sorry if you have regrets that haunt you, and I am sorry that I can't wave a magic wand to allow you to have that conversation one more time. But I can encourage you to change your perspective on how your season looks to you today. Today is what you have, maybe tomorrow, and maybe the next day, but for now, it's today.

> ***So teach us to number our days that we may get a heart of wisdom.***
> Psalm 90:12, ESV

By Guarding What You've Been Given

After you read this chapter, I hope you feel stronger, motivated, and ready to take back your time. Everyone wants a piece of your time, and I hope you share time with many people, but don't forget your time on Earth was given to grow the kingdom. God gifted you with gifts and dreams to spread the gospel and draw people to the cross and resurrection of our Savior. Whenever I open God's word, I see every moment Jesus spent on Earth as intentional, whether it was the woman at the well or calling Zacchaeus down from a tree for dinner. He never allowed temporary pauses in his day to derail Him from a greater purpose. He didn't have to go to Samaria, but He did. He didn't have to call Zacchaeus down from that tree. He could have just waved at him, but He didn't. Jesus made the most of every moment given, and you and I get to choose daily to do the same. Let's look for moments that may seem like an interruption but instead are God's divine intervention and invitation to spread hope to this world.

For me, it was a tough realization paired with a little bit of disobedience. Ok, well, a lot of disobedience. I am an encourager and love motivating people to take bold steps. It's something God has gifted me with, and it makes me so happy when I see people taking steps toward Jesus and using their gifts. That doesn't seem so bad, does it? However, social media is how I encourage people and connect with people, and yet it often starts with a powerful post. Then, 20 minutes later, I am learning how to make a delicious smoothie or scrolling through vacation destinations. What started with good intentions ended with me being distracted and losing some valuable time. I am not by any means calling scrolling a sin, but I am saying that if it consumes your time, and you have little to no room to spend with Jesus or do the things you know you are called to do, then it's a problem. The enemy wants to dangle that delicious carrot out in front of us and prey on what we want so that we no longer see what God has ordained us to do as important. So what do we do? I had to set a timer on my phone to help with how much time I spend on social media. It would tell me I had five more minutes, and for a while, that helped, but eventually, I would hit ignore and keep scrolling. After a few arguments with my husband regarding why there were no clean towels for me and not having things finished for some projects, it hit me that this was a problem. I can blame it on my undiagnosed ADHD, or I can call it what it is. I was being straight-up disobedient, and I had to repent of it.

So, I did just that. I try (really, intentionally try) to no longer scroll. Do I miss Facebook invites? Yes. Do I miss dm's? Yes. Do I miss people announcing things? Yes. I sometimes feel awful when I run into people in public who tell me something they sent me weeks prior. But honestly, I feel at peace in my mind and no longer feel enslaved to a device that can be amazing and defeat me with one swipe. My relationships seem stronger, and the freedom I have is unexplainable. I had a deleting party and an unfollowing party, and together with time management, I truly felt free.

Time is a gift.

Let that settle in. You will never be able to hit a reset button and start over, but you can start at this moment by taking back the time the enemy, the lack of time management, the laziness, or the sin you're dabbling in has stolen from you.

> ***Peace I leave with you; my peace I give to you. Not as the world gives do I give to you. Let not your hearts be troubled, neither let them be afraid.***
> Luke 14:27

I know you desire peace of mind, sweet friend, and I know running toward things that bring comfort is a way you believe that an ounce of peace will come. But goodness, the peace that Jesus brings to our souls doesn't compare to the temporary

By Guarding What You've Been Given

moments of fabricated peace this world offers. Again, please hear me say you have much to give this world. It's time to remove the barriers built up for far too long.

I am no pro at this, but I do love tools to help. So, with that being said, here are some ideas to help you get back your time:

Set a timer on your phone. If you need to do housework, return emails, or make a to-do list, set a timer to keep you on that task. I promise it helps. Don't carry your phone with you from room to room. Set the timer in another room so you must stop to turn it off. There have been so many times I have sat on my bed with my phone to fold a mountain of laundry, and two hours later, I watched a Hallmark movie, and not one piece of laundry got folded. Even at night, I have tried to keep my phone in my bed, but I no longer have it. I will put it on my dresser so that my body can naturally shut down and that melatonin isn't taken by the bright light on my phone.

Another thing that could help is not going to bed with something heavy on your mind. Grab a notebook and write out that thing you don't want to forget to do the following day, or go ahead and make that list of people you want to reach out to. When we think of something, we need to respond at that moment, but sometimes, things must wait. If your mind starts going sixty miles an hour at 11 p.m., get it out on paper, and then go to sleep because IT CAN WAIT. I promise.

Take a few moments before you turn the page and jump into chapter five to pray. One thing I hope you begin to do, if you don't already, is daily repentance. We have to do repentance to set things back in alignment with the Word of God. So, choose to take a moment and repent. Ask God to show you where you're allowing your time to be taken. Sit in that for a few minutes, and then list some things below that seem to take up your time daily (including scrolling through social media or watching Netflix).

Once you have listed a day in your life, I hope you can see that time is a precious gift. We often allow many things to steal moments that could be used for Jesus, rest, or building relationships.

Just today, I was thinking about how badly I wish I could press pause and freeze this moment in time. Watching Rebekah prepare to be a bride and how she enjoys every moment of this wedding planning season is a gift to my soul. But sadly, I can't freeze time. I can, however, allow every moment to be intentional because moments become memories. Memories can also quickly become spiritual marker moments or set off a bomb of regret if we aren't careful. God ordains time with the people you have right now. The time you have right now, either in the valley or on top of that mountain, is ordained by God. God ordains the time you have in the home with your precious toddler. The time you have right now in that job, or in that classroom, or at that college is ordained by God. It is TIME you sit in the moment and soak up the God moments while you can. Take back what the enemy is trying to destroy.

Also, if you need a watch, buy one. Time management is based on our discipline or the lack thereof.

CHAPTER 5

A sweet friendship refreshes the soul.
Proverbs 27:9

Better Together

Guard Your Friendships

This was the most challenging chapter to write. I have lost friendships over my lifetime, but over the last few years, the depth of loss in friendships has been one of the hardest things I have walked through. However, after losing those friendships, the sting lingered for a long time, so it wasn't until now that I could write this without bitterness. I also didn't know what "better together" friendships actually looked like. Over the last few years, God has pulled some pretty ugly things out of me and restored a new love for my community and Biblical, better-together friendships. I know many still friends with their childhood, middle/high school, and college friends. But that's not my story. I have many friends that I keep up with on social media, but I only really keep in touch with less than a handful of those regularly. When I go to God's word about friendship, I see many truths and warnings about the importance of choosing wisely who I let in.

Do not be deceived: "Bad company ruins good morals."
1 Corinthians 15:33, ESV

Even Jesus himself walked with twelve, but Peter, James, and John were on a much deeper level.

Protect What You Cherish

And he allowed no one to follow him except Peter and James and John the brother of James.
Mark 5:37

We opened a pool a few years ago, and over the last two years, I have been in that pool four or five times. It's right outside my back door, yet the heat often keeps me away, even though I know the pool will bring me coolness and refreshment. Sometimes, it's simply because I don't want to get my hair wet, because I wash it once every week or so, so I miss out on the rest the pool could bring. I have to literally take a few steps through the heat to step into relief. Y'all, my pool in my backyard goes unused on a lot of days.

So many of us have people surrounding us who are ready and willing to dive into a deeper friendship, but because we have our eyes on another friendship or the fear of what could happen if we allow ourselves to be vulnerable, we miss out. We can also become so caught up in the number of friends that we can miss the depth of Biblical community. Likes drive social media, and because of that, we have an expectation of what friendship is supposed to look like, and it couldn't be further off. That's why we still feel lonely, left out, and desiring depth. Let me free you. It's not about making a post with that one friend who you think will help you grow in social stature, nor is it about the number of friends you possess. I am not a friendship expert, but I desire it, and I know how important it is to have people championing me and speaking the truth in my life. In Exodus 17, Aaron gives us a glimpse into what it looks like to be a better-together friend.

11 Whenever Moses held up his hand, Israel prevailed, and whenever he lowered his hand, Amalek prevailed. 12 But Moses' hands grew weary, so they took a stone and put it under him, and he sat on it, while Aaron and Hur held up his hands, one on one side, and the other on the other side.

By Guarding What You've Been Given

So his hands were steady until the going down of the sun.
Exodus 17:11-12 ESV

That last line gets me every single time.

"So his hands were steady until the going down of the sun."

Imagine being so tired you can't even lift your arms, and even further, the battle depended on Moses keeping his hands raised, yet his physical strength was waning due to his old age. I may not be old age, but there have been seasons in my life where I truly believed I would not make it through. I am good at wearing a mask of "I am okay," and yet the people who are incredibly in tune with who I truly am would always reach in and begin to hold my arms up. Not physically, but sometimes it was just me crying on the phone, and other times, it was coming to help me with my girls or help clean my house. No matter how small or big the gesture was, I felt my strength restored simply because of their intentionality and willingness to be present and strong when I didn't feel strong.

Maybe, as you read the words on this page, you can feel loneliness rising in you. You have wished and prayed for someone to come alongside you to help you walk through this season. First, I want to say Jesus is and wants to be that friend to you. He is forever in your corner. He carries you through the seasons where your legs can barely stand. He holds up your arms when you can't seem to muster up a single hallelujah, and His Word is very clear that He draws near to the brokenhearted, which is so special, because He promises to be with us; he must lean in even more to where we are on the days we feel so broken.

The Lord is near to the brokenhearted and saves the crushed in spirit.
Psalm 34:18

Second, I encourage you to reach out to people. Sometimes, our pride gets in the way, and it's easier to be offended and feel "left out" when, in reality, some people are waiting for your invitation. Today, maybe it's time you pick up the phone and text a few people with encouragement. Then, set up at least one (or two) lunch or coffee dates. But please don't choose to do nothing. Remember, friendship will never be one-sided.

Better-together friendships will always remind you of two things:
1. Who God is.
2. Who you are in Christ.

If your friendship is only filled with fun activities or shallow conversations, it will never experience the depth of a true, genuine connection. Friendship requires truth, grace, and a constant reminder of Jesus, even when our seasons are hard.

I remember becoming a brand new believer in my freshman year of college. I honestly thought I would immediately feel and be different. However, some things did change, like how I looked at my relationship with Richard. I no longer desired to be physical with him in ways that didn't honor Jesus. I had to put firm boundaries in place by replacing those moments that could lead us back into temptation with things like board games, movies, or going for a ride in the car. The desire didn't go away immediately, but my actions to those desires changed drastically. Also, the music I was listening to began to change because things that once had my attention no longer did. It was a daily step in surrender and repentance daily. Another big area that began to change was my friendships. I began to desire people who were pursuing the things of Jesus over partying and satisfying the desires of the flesh. One by one, God began to put new people into my life while other friendships fell away. There was no big fight or disagreement; it was just a natural divide. I wanted friends with purpose for the first time in my life. I wanted people in my life who would teach me a new way of living, including pointing me to Jesus when I didn't. They would ask me about spending time in the Word and invite me into deeper conversations about what it looked like to follow Jesus. I spent my life, up until that point, trying so hard to please everyone with what I wore, how I talked, and the things I was interested in. It wasn't until I met people who loved me for me (flaws and all) that I began to see such beauty in those friendships. The truth is that "better-together" friendships will never make you second guess who you are, push you away from truth, or make you feel empty or distant from Jesus. (If that happens, that's a red flag.)

Once you establish this type of community, it takes more than a weekly coffee date, phone date, or Instagram shoutout to keep it alive and thriving. It takes intentionality. The same goes for protecting those types of friendships.

One way to guard your friendships is never to choose the passive-aggressive path. That means comments on social media or to others simply because you're frustrated or hurt by them. If you're upset with them, tell them you are upset, but don't make them feel a certain way simply because you don't choose to address the problem. If they aren't willing to fix it or at least have a hard conversation, then maybe that friendship isn't what you thought it was to begin with. Goodness, I have been in that place, and it stings. I have been friends with people and then suddenly realized they had unfollowed me or blocked my number, but never once was a conversation offered. Did I do something? Maybe so, but I will never know because no conversation happened, which is unfair.

Another way to guard your friendships is to allow them to speak truth into your life.

I have a friend, Lauren, who is also a pastor's wife and speaker, and when I need truth without any fluff (sandwiched with some encouragement), she is my go-to. She never holds back, but I trust her because she walks with Jesus. She doesn't fear losing my friendship because it's built on Jesus. That may sound cheesy, but it's the truth. We can laugh hysterically on the phone and cry, and she has never made me wonder if she was for me. She speaks hard truths to me, and I am better because of it. I remember one time, I was walking through a tough season in ministry, and I wanted to explode on someone. I went to social media and typed a long post, but the Holy Spirit said NO WAY, so I deleted it before I posted it. However, what I did was just as petty. I literally typed the laughing face emoji, and beside it, I wrote, "hahahahahaha." Within minutes, Lauren texted me, saying, "Take that down." I knew the person I wanted to see wouldn't actually see it, but I needed to vent, and yet, that was the wrong response because my intent was wrong. Lauren reminded me of the truth, and I took it down. She guarded my heart, ministry, and mind with Biblical truth. She let me say why I was mad, she listened, and then she said, "Let it go." Lauren has never been passive with me. Such a gift is choosing to surround yourself with people (or someone) who will never let you settle for bitterness or apathy. Biblical community requires you to reach out and allows others to reach in. When you allow that friendship to be cemented in truth first, your friendships will be stronger because of it (I promise).

Another way to guard your friendships is to be willing to stay even when you want to run.

Another of my best friends, Nicki (also a pastor's wife), and I went to Texas for the If-gathering, and from the moment we arrived in Texas, it was adventure after adventure. She booked us a hotel (I hold that word loosely) for a lower price, and y'all, there were blood stains on the floor and a creepy hand print going across the mirror. I can't make this stuff up. We are two people who love true crime, so the stories we made up in that room were so funny but also creeped me out a wee bit. On top of that, the elevator was broken, so we had to walk up four flights of stairs every single time we wanted to leave. Part of me wanted to say forget it; let's just move to a new hotel, but the other part loved its chaos and adventure. Nicki and I would run down the hall and quickly down the stairs in case someone tried to grab us. On this same trip, we purchased tickets to a pop-up. If you don't know what that is, google pop-ups will suddenly show all kinds of things that come up. Basically, they are experiences that are only offered for a short time.

Most are interactive and offer a lot of great photo ops. This one, however, started with us banging on the door, trying to get someone to let us in. After a good, long while, we were welcomed by a guy in a rainbow suit who may or may not have been high. He told us the parameters of the pop-up and then cut us loose. I was 100% convinced this was a hoax, but nevertheless, we proceeded. We laughed so much and took some pictures with many cool backgrounds. However, the last room was the surprise of the whole thing. We walked in, and as the door shut, there was suddenly weirdly dim lighting. Elevator music was playing, and we saw what looked to be clouds made of huge cotton balls and a hot air balloon. Now, this sounds quite magical, but for my claustrophobic self, it was a nightmare. I took the picture and suddenly started looking for the door so I knew I could get out. I needed that exit door opened, and Nicki helped me find it quickly. As we walked out, laughing at the whole thing, I was reminded that friends who don't exit when things are hard or uncomfortable are friends worth fighting for. We must stop the "unfollow" movement based on our feelings getting hurt. Instead, we need to start having hard conversations. We need to say hard things, receive hard things, and then choose to stay.

Since 2010, when God called Richard and I to plant Revolution Church, people have come and gone for various reasons. I have realized that through the hard seasons, those who remained through the good, bad, and the ugly are MY PEOPLE. I'm not talking about the ones who were called to go or do something else. I still deeply love those people, but I am talking about those who were offended but never said they were. The ones who didn't like a decision made but never said they didn't. The ones who complained to everyone but wouldn't actually help. Think about it this way: when we choose to walk out of someone's life due to anger, hurt, or our own hard season, what are we actually telling them? Are we saying that their friendship is worth fighting for?

It wasn't until after great loss that I began to check my own heart, my words, and my actions. Do I wish I could go back and say some things? 100% yes. Guarding your friendships will always require your own self-inventory moments, moments where you look in the mirror and ask yourself the hard questions. It's self-awareness of how you treat your friendships publicly and behind closed doors. Are you posting all the social media pics to maintain an image of a friendship simply because you think you need it to remain relevant or cool? When, in all actuality, that is not cool at all. Those types of moments create such a false sense of genuine friendship. I always tell girls struggling with friendship to ask themselves what they can do, too. (Yes, I said too). If we think it's just the other person's responsibility to carry and maneuver the hard seasons of friendship, then maybe we aren't a better friend together after all, and maybe we are a part of the problem. When I look into God's Word, I see such beauty in David and Jonathan's friendship. Let's take a look.

As soon as he had finished speaking to Saul, the soul of Jonathan was knit to the soul of David, and Jonathan loved him as his own soul.
1 Samuel 18:18, ESV

The description behind the word knit is defined by Vine's Expository dictionary as this: "to cause to coalesce, to join or knit together."[10] Think about the blanket your grandmother

By Guarding What You've Been Given

knit you or the one you bought at Target simply because it felt cozy. Every strand was woven together perfectly. This is how I read those words: "knit to the soul." It was a God-ordained friendship destined to be, and it taught me so much about friendship. Think about the people you call friends. Do you feel that way about them? Do you feel like God created that friendship? Did that person come after a desperate prayer for deeper friendships? Did that group of friends seek you out? Did you click with someone at an event? The reality is God ordains people in every season of our lives; some stay for the next season, and some we must let go.

We have to protect and choose those who decide to stay. We must listen to them and allow God to cultivate a beautiful friendship. I love what Jonathan did for David in 1 Samuel 18.

18 As soon as he had finished speaking to Saul, the soul of Jonathan was knit to the soul of David, and Jonathan dloved him as his own soul. 2 And Saul took him that day eand would not let him return to his father's house. 3 Then Jonathan made a covenant with David, because dhe loved him as his own soul. 4 And Jonathan stripped himself of the robe that was on him and gave it to David, and his armor, and even his sword and his bow and his belt. 5 And David went out fand was successful wherever Saul sent him, so that Saul set him over the men of war. And this was good in the sight of all the people and also in the sight of Saul's servants.
1 Samuel 18:1-5, NIV

Jonathan took their friendship seriously. It wasn't for publicity or personal gain. So many times, I believe that the idea of status or thought that someone can do something for you can creep up, and we lose sight of the weight and seriousness of friendship. For Jonathon, it was based on his deep love for David because it wasn't a hobby that connected them; it was the spirit of God. The second thing I see is that Jonathan gave David a few things.

1. His robe
2. Armor
3. A sword
4. A bow
5. A belt

The things meant to protect and help him fight were the things he released to help protect and guard David. His robe tells of his status and his royalty, yet he places it on David. Do you see your friends the way God sees them? Do you treat them with respect, loyalty, and honor?

Secondly, the armor reminds me of battle. Do you go to battle in prayer for your friendships? Do you run to the battle line for them or towards them when things get hard? The sword and the bow are both weapons. For our friendships, we have to give them truth so they can see circumstances, seasons, and themselves with new eyes. Truth cuts through the shallow and says, "I SEE YOU, and I will clothe you in who God has purposed you to be." The belt reminds me of how it holds everything together. God holds your friendships together when they are rooted in Him. Our friendships are extensions of His goodness, and our words, prayers, and intentionality are how friendships deepen and grow.

The friends who weren't afraid to speak up when pride was rearing its ugly head or my fears were taking me in the opposite direction of obedience were the friends who chose to clothe me when I couldn't see beyond the pain or the circumstance.

Before I end this chapter, I also want to press pause on the friendships that end, the ones where harsh words were spoken, or maybe nothing was said, yet you knew that friendship

By Guarding What You've Been Given

needed to end. The reality is that if two people are going in different directions, it's a natural release. If you walk into a room and feel the room shift because of words spoken before you entered, it's okay to let those friendships go. We can love people from a distance and not be best friends with them. The pain my heart has felt over the last 15 years within the ministry is a pain I do not want others ever to experience. I had some sleepless nights, yet I bet the people who spoke those words about me didn't lose an ounce of sleep. But I know that releasing them was a part of healing my heart and allowing other people to step in and be a part of that healing. Have I hurt people with my words? Of course. I have also chosen to repent, pray for that person, and guard my current friendships with such caution.

Better together friendships,
Will not tear you down
  - Instead, they will always lift you and speak life into you.

Will not make you beg for their attention.
  - Instead, they will choose you, even when people are looking.

Will not make you strive to be someone you are not.
  - Instead, they will fan the flame God has put into you and cheer you on.

Will not allow others to talk about you when you're not around.
  - Instead, they will always speak up for you and shut down the gossip.

Will not make you feel insecure.
  - Instead, they will remind you of who you are in Christ.

When you understand that friendship is a gift, you begin to cherish it from a new perspective.
I have been friends with a few ladies for almost two decades.

Protect What You Cherish

I have several friendships that were birthed from a deeper place that only God could have knit together. I have never felt more sure that genuine forever friendships are not seasonal. I will protect those friendships at all costs and choose them with my words and my actions in all seasons not just when it's convenient. My friends that are beyond the surface level conversation have been cultivated by God in the spirit, and I am forever grateful. I also know that if one of us speaks out of a place of defeat, fear, insecurity, or pain we immediately send encouragement and truth. We use Bible verses and intentional words that uplift and move the soul. My closest friends have nothing to do with gaining a social status and everything to do with a bond that will never be broken. Friend, if you desire this type of friendship, believe you're worthy and trust God has your best in mind. My best friends in this season didn't happen overnight; they were cultivated over years, deep conversations, hard talks, and prayer, and some of them I rarely see. Friendship is meant to refresh your soul, not deplete it. Recently, I was at the lake with some of my very best friends, and my mentor, Debbie, and I sat back and just listened to the conversations happening. My heart couldn't help but thank God for each of them. From Rachael praying for and with me to always finding ways to encourage me, we cry together, read God's Word together, and just sit together, and it's beautiful.

One of the hardest parts of friendships is feeling chosen for so many girls. I get it, sweet friend; I truly do. I started praying for friendships that would edify the body and push me closer to Jesus. God gifted me with those types of friendships. Ariel is one of those friends who chooses me constantly. She chooses to sit with me on a Sunday morning, but she also chooses to sit with me on the couch to watch a movie and say nothing. No matter what environment we are in, she always chooses me, and I can't tell you how that makes me feel. For years, I felt as if I was the last choice, and having a best friend like Ariel has been a gift to me. (Thank you, Ariel, for choosing me.)

By Guarding What You've Been Given

Before you move on to the next chapter, I want you to do two things.

First, pray for your friendships.

Call them out by name, and thank God for what they bring to your life. My friends are all so different, and all hold a different purpose in my life. God has woven them like that beautiful, cozy blanket I mentioned earlier to cover me in this season of my life.

As you pray for them, pray for their minds and hearts to be protected, and ask God to use your words to help protect and guard their hearts.

Second, I want you to seek someone new.

Ask God to show you who needs you in this season. Then, text them and ask them to coffee or come over for dinner. Be open to new friendships, and let other people into your current friendships. You have so much to give, and so do your friends, so don't be a gatekeeper.

The enemy wants to keep division in the church, in your schools, and your workplaces, and he will stop at nothing to keep you insecure and feeling like you aren't good enough in the friendships you are in. I wish I could go back to conversations I had with people early in ministry and fix issues that were never addressed, but I can't. I have learned that the hard way, and because of my unwillingness, I have lost people in seasons that I never expected. The reality is some friendships only last a season, but recognizing the friendships that bring glory to God while also refreshing my soul has helped me not only nurture my current friendships with new eyes but also recognize where I fall short within those same friendships. Miscommunication indeed keeps a lot of people from ever moving past the shallow conversations, but also, withholding hard conversations can keep your friendships at arm's length. We have to get over our pride in letting people in, or we will lean in the direction of loneliness and isolation and blame people for it. Maybe you're reading this, and you're thinking, "Holly, I don't trust anyone because I keep getting hurt." Please hear me say I am sorry, and I don't think we are ever meant to become doormats for people within friendships. But also, hear me say those people who keep hurting you may not be the people you need to be friends with. Do you love them? Absolutely. But allowing them to walk in and out of every season? NO.

Better together friendships are not about shaping who they want you to be. They're about complimenting each other while sharpening one another in the process so you both look more like Christ. When you have a healthy perspective of friendship, I promise you will begin to see those people differently. In your mind, you may think you need them to survive, and that's not true. Jesus does the opening and shutting of doors, and He fills the void you're longing to fill.

> ***For He satisfies the longing soul,***
> ***and the hungry soul He fills with good things.***
> Psalm 107:9, ESV

Only Jesus can satisfy our souls. Only Jesus.

Or, you may think there is no one with whom you can fully connect. That is not true. But maybe it will take you stepping away from friendships that are suffocating you, isolating you, and keeping you in a place of chasing their approval to see the people God is placing in front of you. Sometimes, it truly takes stepping back or away to see things with fresh eyes. So many people are chasing after approval, they can't see the friendships they are in aren't growing them in any way, and it's because they are like a hamster on a wheel running and striving to keep a friendship from dissolving when, in reality, you need to let go so you can grow.

By Guarding What You've Been Given

A Biblical community doesn't always mean they become your best friends. Let that sink in for a moment. Just because you're sitting in the same lifegroup, Sunday school, college dorm room, or on the same row at your church doesn't mean you are going to be close friends, and you need to be okay with that. It is true that sometimes beautiful friendships bloom out of those things, but not always. I love the people within my church, and I call those my people and my community, but do I hang out with all of them on a regular basis? No, and that is okay. Some of my closest friends are people who live in other states. They are also pastors' wives that understand my journey. They get the hard parts and rejoice in the good parts. They just get it, and they each make me better in their own way. If I'm honest, those far-away friendships have encouraged me more often than those around me in some seasons, and I am okay with that. It took me a long time to say that out loud, but I am okay with that. In that season, I learned to tell those around me what I needed, and that changed many of those friendships. Everyone deserves deeper friendships, and just because you may not be in a friendship group that you want doesn't mean you are being rejected. It may just mean you need to find new friends.

I know this chapter may rub many of you the wrong way, and that's not my intent at all. I hope it does the opposite. I want you to feel free within your friendships. I want you to be able to do what you are called to do with people surrounding you, cheering you on, challenging you, and holding you accountable without resentment, bitterness, or competition. Those things stifle and stop friendships from blooming. When you begin to surround yourself with people who love you with their words and their actions, you will want to keep those people around.

Maybe your personality clashes with another person. That doesn't mean you must push them away, not like them, or change who you are. It simply means you may need to love them from the perspective of a Biblical community and not a deep friendship. I believe we have such a distorted view of friendship that, when someone rubs us the wrong way, we stiff-arm them and run in the opposite direction.

I have sat in circles where someone has driven me bonkers, even to the point I would dodge her on a Sunday morning. Still, after stopping for a moment, I realize God created them completely different than me, and even more, their upbringing shaped them in a way that was foreign to me and kept me from seeing them fully.

I didn't truly see her because I didn't want to. I remember stopping on a Sunday morning to hug her, and she asked me for a coffee date. I dreaded it all the way up until the moment I was walking into the coffee shop. I sat listening to her talk, and I could almost feel my heart melting. I had stiff-armed someone simply because they got on my nerves, and yet this woman in front of me was vulnerable, transparent, and deeply wounded from her childhood. Her personality was like nails on a chalkboard, but her willingness to connect was something I lacked, and that kept me from letting her in.

After that coffee date, I returned to my car, feeling like a jerk. I didn't become best friends with her because we don't click, but I see her in a new way, even today. I don't dread seeing her coming my way because I now see her as someone in my season that God loves, cherishes, and pursues, just like He does me. The people who make your eyes twitch as soon as you see their name pop up on your phone may just be an assignment from God, so don't let pride or preference get in the way.

Take a moment and pray for your friendships in this season. Ask God to strengthen them, but then, take a moment and write out a prayer of repentance. The people you keep putting off, stiff-arming, and refusing to let in are also in your season, ordained

By Guarding What You've Been Given

by God, and though they may not be your better-together people, they are God's people. Just like they are in your season on purpose, you are also in their season on purpose.

I will touch on friendship later, but I want you to live fully in freedom by enjoying the deepest friendships, even now. Just because someone says they are for you doesn't mean they are with you, which is okay. However, when you find those "for you" and "with you" friends, you do whatever you can to protect them.

To build the kingdom by building His body with your words and actions today, and encourage your friends by sending them a text or a coffee gift card (who doesn't love those?!).

Protect What You Cherish

CHAPTER 6

And your ears shall hear a word behind you, saying, "This is the way, walk in it," when you turn to the right or when you turn to the left.
Isaiah 30:21

Guard the Truth.

Mama Bear Mode

I remember when I was in youth group, and my youth pastor placed chairs, tables, and books all over the floor around the room. He placed blindfolds over our eyes and had us choose to listen to the crowd screaming which way to walk or, instead, listen to his voice as he stood close, speaking softly in our ears about which way we should turn or when to take a bigger step. It was hard to hear his voice because many people were yelling. I could listen to my friends' voices so much easier, yet deep down, I knew Pastor Rex was telling me the truth.

In this chapter, I want to dive into the next thing God has given us to guard: truth. God's Word is the only truth. The world has made it clear it no longer believes God's Word is true; even more, the enemy is distorting it, and sadly, people are believing him. But His Word is true, and unless you believe fully, it will be up for debate in your soul and mind until you eventually no longer see clearly or want to obey what it says.

And no wonder, for even Satan disguises himself as an angel of light.
2 Corinthians 11:14, ESV

Protect What You Cherish

The number of times I have heard "my truth" statements over the last few years has blown my mind. For some people, it's their way of conveying a personal story of pain or heartache; to them, it's what they know to be true. I'm not talking about that. I *am* talking about when we allow our circumstances, preferences, feelings, and desires to trump God's Word and call it "truth." Our feelings seem to get in the way a lot. When a breakup happens or something doesn't go as planned, we tend to bend toward the direction of emotion over God's Word. The enemy begins to prey on our emotions. Before too long, we justify, explain away, or no longer even go to God's Word looking for clarity because deep down, we don't believe it's true to our circumstances, so we lean into this idea that "my truth" is absolute.

When I began writing this book seven years ago, I didn't even have this chapter as a part of my outline. But now, seven years later, seeing how the enemy has stolen and distorted God's truth, and after losing people to new ideologies and watching person after person begin to question the validity of scripture, it stirred something in me. I knew I must learn what it meant to guard my heart and mind in the process because I had to wrestle and choose to believe what God's Word says and believe it wholeheartedly. For years, people have used the excuse, "I don't have time to read my Bible," but now, anyone can scroll on TikTok and see a pretty girl with some soft music playing while holding crystals, quote scripture out of context, and people believe it.

That is the "why" behind this chapter. I have to help in some way, and if it's just you reading this chapter and becoming aware, for the first time, that guarding the truth requires you to be in the Word of God, then awesome. But it also may be that you have found yourself in some deep unbelief, and the enemy has tainted the Word of God in your mind, and you are hanging on by a thread. If that is you, then please keep going.

By Guarding What You've Been Given

God wants you to know His Word sets us free. His Word brings true healing, peace, clarity, and hope amid our messes and wrestling.

Sweet friend, hear me say keep going and keep reading, but more than that, choose to shut down the voices that are competing for your heart and mind. If the voices speaking into your life don't align with the Word of God, then what is being communicated is NOT true.

> ***The sum of your word is truth,***
> ***and every one of your righteous rules endures forever.***
> Psalm 119:160, ESV

You can trust every word of the Bible is true. You can trust His word will give you tools and weapons to fight against the enemy's schemes. Ephesians 6 is a reminder of this truth.

> ***Finally, be strong in the Lord and in the strength of his might.***
> ***Put on the whole armor of God, that you may be able to***
> ***stand against the schemes of the devil.***
> Ephesians 6:10-11

When you have a headache, you take headache medicine. If you have a dental issue, you go to the dentist. But why is it that when there is a profound soul question or longing, we don't turn to Jesus? I am not pointing fingers at you, I promise, because there have been plenty of times when I have run straight to a friend or, sadly, even to food to give me comfort or what I needed in that moment of spiraling. But there have also been times I have felt lonely, deep grief, rejection, sadness, and a whole lot of other emotions I took to Jesus and no one else. I allowed myself time to sit with the Father and to soak up His Word. Sometimes, I experienced a season of those things before I saw and felt change. Other times, I felt immediate release or relief. God's Word clearly brings change in our lives, and it's up to me to believe it, receive it, and walk fully in the truth God has placed in front of me.

For the word of God is living and active, sharper than any two-edged sword, piercing to the division of soul and of spirit, of joints and of marrow, and discerning the thoughts and intentions of the heart.
Hebrews 4:12, ESV

I want to change gears for a moment and discuss our friend Ehud in Judges Chapter 3. When I started writing this book, I honestly thought the entire book would be focused on his story alone. What I didn't know was how God was going to stretch me. I tried many times to make it work in my head and on paper, but then I realized it wasn't for the entire book but for this chapter alone. The sword Ehud used to kill the king, to his uniqueness of being left-handed, was all a part of God's perfect plan. Ehud had to respond in obedience but also not hesitate. Let's look back at the verses in Judges 3. As you read this, I want you to imagine this amazing story. I honestly would love to see a cartoon of this one day; I mean, It's funny, but also packed full of truth and encouragement for our souls.

Okay, let's read:

12 And the people of Israel again did what was evil in the sight of the Lord, and the Lord strengthened Eglon the king of Moab against Israel, because they had done what was evil in the sight of the Lord. 13 He gathered to himself the Ammonites and the Amalekites, and went and defeated Israel. And they took possession of the city of palms. 14 And the people of Israel served Eglon the king of Moab eighteen years. 15 Then the people of Israel cried out to the Lord, and <u>the Lord raised up for them a deliverer, Ehud</u>, the son of Gera, the Benjaminite, a left-handed man. The people of Israel sent tribute by him to Eglon the king of Moab. 16 And Ehud made for himself a sword with two edges, a

By Guarding What You've Been Given

cubit[a] in length, and he bound it on his right thigh under his clothes. 17 And he presented the tribute to Eglon king of Moab. Now Eglon was a very fat man. 18 And when Ehud had finished presenting the tribute, he sent away the people who carried the tribute. 19 But he himself turned back at the idols near Gilgal and said, "I have a secret message for you, O king." And he commanded, "Silence." And all his attendants went out from his presence. 20 And Ehud came to him as he was sitting alone in his cool roof chamber. And Ehud said, "I have a message from God for you." And he arose from his seat. 21 <u>And Ehud reached with his left hand, took the sword from his right thigh, and thrust it into his belly. 22 And the hilt also went in after the blade, and the fat closed over the blade, for he did not pull the sword out of his belly; and the dung came out.</u> 23 Then Ehud went out into the porch[b] and closed the doors of the roof chamber behind him and locked them. 24 When he had gone, the servants came, and when they saw that the doors of the roof chamber were locked, they thought, "Surely he is relieving himself in the closet of the cool chamber." 25 And they waited till they were embarrassed. But when he still did not open the doors of the roof chamber, they took the key and opened them, and there lay their lord dead on the floor. 26 Ehud escaped while they delayed, and he passed beyond the idols and escaped to Seirah. 27 When he arrived, he sounded the trumpet in the hill country of Ephraim. Then the people of Israel went down with him from the hill country, and he was their leader. 28 And he said to them, "Follow after me, for the Lord has given your enemies the Moabites into your hand." So they went down after him and seized the fords of the Jordan against the Moabites and did not allow anyone to pass over. 29 And they killed at that time about 10,000 of the Moabites, all strong, able-bodied men; not a man escaped. 30 So Moab was subdued that day under the hand of Israel. And the land had rest for eighty years.

Judges 3:12-30

Protect What You Cherish

Now, I know that's a lot of scripture, but wow, right? Every part of this story led to peace for a lot of people. I know I mentioned this before, but my goodness, Ehud's obedience to God brought peace to the land for eighty years. That is a very long time. Imagine what your obedience may bring to the next generation? Or the generation after? If we know our weapon is God's Word and that it will cause us to do hard things for the kingdom's sake, we must first understand what it says. So, how do we protect God's Word from being distorted? Ehud could have hesitated easily when he stepped into the King's quarters. He could have second-guessed the call to go, but instead, he stood firm in His loyalty to God above all else. When we are seeking God's truth for our hearts, there are a few things I want to encourage you with.

First, you have to **receive** it.

When a small child needs discipline, and a mama responds with words of direction, they stop the behavior because they know mama means business. I will never understand, however, when a mama uses the 1-2-3 method, but you hear them on 9 or 10 in the warning. Knowing the parent will not follow through with the punishment, that kid doesn't receive their warnings.

Sadly, we are the same with allowing God to have full authority over our lives. We say we want Him to reign, yet we stiff-arm Him when what we want doesn't align with His Word. Do you believe God's Word is true and accurate? If so, ask yourself if you accept it as full authority over every area of your life. Receiving it is letting it in, opening His Word, and sitting with it. The Holy Spirit does the rest, but there is active participation on our part in picking up the Word of God. His Word is the only truth, which means we must be careful of what we allow to creep in through all the other avenues, from social media to friendships to sad music and movies. Bending or distorting the truth is easy to follow if we aren't careful.

Secondly, we have to **believe** it.

We can read something all day and yet do the opposite of what it says. Paul talked about it in Romans 7.

> *15 For I do not understand my own actions. For I do not do what I want, but I do the very thing I hate. 16 Now if I do what I do not want, I agree with the law, that it is good. 17 So now it is no longer I who do it, but sin that dwells within me. 18 For I know that nothing good dwells in me, that is, in my flesh. For I have the desire to do what is right, but not the ability to carry it out. 19 For I do not do the good I want, but the evil I do not want is what I keep on doing. 20 Now if I do what I do not want, it is no longer I who do it, but sin that dwells within me.*
> Romans 7:15-20

It is like a pull between the flesh and God's truth. But the moment we are torn between delighting in the desires we know don't align with God's Word, we have entered a dangerous place. We risk eventually blurring the lines of what is truth and what is not. If there is a trace of a lie, it's not the truth. We all know certain things have the potential to harm us, and yet, we ignore the warning signs. For instance, how many years have we been warned about the damage of sun exposure? I had skin cancer early in my twenties, and it took me into my forties to now lather myself in sunscreen. The same goes with flirting with the desires of the flesh, and the same goes with unbelief. It creeps up into spaces we didn't even see coming. We often want to believe it, but because our souls have neglected truth for far too long, we allow other voices in, and then we don't know what we believe or why we even believe it. If there is one thing I can encourage you to do, it is never to stop reading your Bible. Don't exchange God's Word for the world's imitation of what it is trying to convey.

Take a second or two and write below a few things you may be currently wrestling with. Writing it out lets you see the wrestling within from a different perspective. It also allows you to write out some Biblical truth besides those things that cause unrest in your mind. Is it a hot topic you see circulating all over social media, and you have no idea what the Bible says about it? Or maybe, it's some thing you only know what your friends say about them, your parents, or TikTok. I believe when you are confused, it's time to not only wrestle with those things; it's a choice to allow the Light in. The beauty of God's Word is it will not bring confusion into that place; it will only bring clarity. ***God's Word brings us closer to the heart of God while also revealing His holiness.*** When you hold up the "thing" that keeps tripping you up under the light of God's Word, you will begin to see it with new eyes. Because darkness and light cannot co-exist, we either run to darkness out of shame and hide as Adam and Eve did in the garden, or we run towards the light, repent, and allow God's truth to be what sets our feet back on sturdy ground.

The foundation of our souls is where we have to begin.

If you attend church weekly, try not to cuss or have sex "outside of marriage," and find yourself in a place of following rules, then you probably don't realize the validity of God's Word and the power it can have in your life. When you allow your soul to embrace God's Word as the only truth, it exposes any competing opinions, lies, or desires that don't align with His Word.

I have had seasons where I chased the idea I could follow God with my behavior, and it was not attached to a place of surrender or deep-rooted faith. I read my Bible as a chore; I went to church because I was supposed to, and, if I am honest, that season felt like the biggest drought. It felt like I was drawing from an empty well, and the truth is, I was. The problem with wrestling isn't in the wrestling, or even the unbelief; it's in the

By Guarding What You've Been Given

response to it. Either I back away from what I know to be true and choose my own way, or I choose God's way. I have also walked through hard seasons where I felt like I saw no trace of God in my prayer life, nor in my quiet times with Him, yet the intimacy I felt was unmatched. I believe the difference was I believed His Word to be true, and I chose not to move until I heard His voice on a matter I had taken to Him over and over and over again.

Have you ever sat outside and watched the birds? I personally love it. I love it when May rolls around. For one, it's my birthday month, and it also means the weather is perfect. I get many gifts (my love language is gifts), and I get to celebrate all the fun things all month. But it's also when it's no longer too cold to sit outside in the mornings for quiet time. I remember sitting outside one morning when the pool cover was off, and the water seemed like a sheet of glass. The birds were chirping louder than usual, and the wind blew through my hair and across my face as if someone was standing beside me, fanning me. The bluest bluejay landed on the pool's edge as I looked up and found myself in what felt like a beautiful symphony of nature in my backyard. This bird, y'all, leaned over, lifted his body slowly, flew just close enough to get some water, and then flew away quickly. It was as if the stillness of the water drew him to it. I immediately felt Jesus remind me of the verse in Psalm 42:

"As the deer pants for streams of water, so my soul pants for you, my God. My soul thirsts for God, for the living God. When can I go and meet with God?"
Psalm 42:1-2, NIV

The image of a deer standing on the side of a stream, panting as if his life depended on a sip of water, is the image God gave me at that moment with this beautiful blue bird. I then went there for myself. Does my soul thirst for the living God? Do I seek fulfillment fully in Him? Do I truly desire nothing more, or, even more, do I believe He is what brings soul satisfaction to the dry and desperate areas? Because sweet friend, I will eventually stop going to the water's edge if I don't believe it. Please hear my heart on this. I stopped seeking God for a season or two or three and sought after food, perfection, and approval to fulfill, and when I was younger, I sought it with the affection of a boy. Looking back across those seasons, the reality and common denominator was that my heart reflected my belief. I didn't believe that God would satisfy me. I am sitting at my kitchen table currently, and it's the middle of May. I am a few days away from my daughter getting engaged, my charcuterie-themed birthday party, and a one-day trip to Disney with my best friend, and though those are all fantastic things, there is a deep-rooted longing for more within me. But not for more things, more money, or even more adventure; it's a longing to be with the Father. (Okay, so now I am crying.) Y'all, these tears tell the story of where my heart has been and where it is now. My heart longs to know God for more than reading His name on a picture or the screen in worship or across a page of a book or in the bible. He is the God who knows my deepest desires and still chooses to stay with me. He knows when my thoughts steer toward pride, selfishness, and disobedience and chooses to stay with me. He knows when my feet are slowly moving in the direction of sin, and He knows when my words don't depict His character, BUT He chooses to stay, and He still wants me. The God of the Bible is a personal God that created you, and in knowing that, we should stumble through this life, always in need of His power to help us stand firm. He knew it, and He sent His son to die on our behalf so we didn't have to walk in defeat or stay defeated.

How do I know this? Please don't take my word for it.

For God so loved the world that He gave His only son, that whosoever believes in Him shall not perish but have everlasting life.
John 3:16, NIV

By Guarding What You've Been Given

Many believers can quote this verse, yet I truly think many don't actually believe. Do they believe that Jesus died on the cross? Yes. Do they believe that Heaven is real? Yes. But do they (you and me) also trust in a deep-rooted belief that Jesus is the ONLY way to heaven and the only way to truth?

Sometimes, we just don't seem to trust in His sovereignty because we tend to stop seeking His Word for guidance, clarity, wisdom, and healing the moment we get uncomfortable in our seasons, someone offends us, or we aren't "feeling it." Instead, we run to the things or people that enslave us to new ideologies. This new wave of "TikTok" theology I mentioned earlier in the chapter has derailed so many people from what truth is to the point of them walking away from their faith altogether. Additionally, some have now mixed a little bit of this spirituality with a little bit of this and that from other religions, and even witchcraft, and sadly believe it's all truth.

I hope that everyone who reads this chapter is strengthened in their faith. I hope you will align your beliefs not with what my culture or I say but instead with what the Word of God says. Remember, if you want to Google any stance, opinion, or side on any topic, you will always find what you want to match your feelings. But also remember that the Word of God cuts deep, and it isn't to hurt you but to transform you to be more like Christ. His Word sets you free, redeems you, and removes shame and guilt. No one else's words can do that for you. That truth alone makes me want to know His Word even more.

At one point in my life, I was that friend who only told you what you wanted to hear. I wanted you to like me, and I didn't want to cause a rift in our friendship. Whether it be something about what you were wearing or something about your relationship, I leaned into the direction you were headed because I wanted you to feel close to me regardless of how I truly felt or what I knew to be true. The older I become, the more I read God's word, and I realize how terrible that is when it comes to any relationship or friendship. If we believe iron truly sharpens iron, as the Bible says, I have to tell the truth regardless of how awkward that may be. Truth aligns with the Word of God, not my feelings or the other person's. This idea of "my truth" is not truth; it's only opinions masked by what you want or believe to be true.

I can argue with you that Coke Zero is better than Diet Coke. But if you are a diehard Diet Coke girl, nothing will steer you into believing that what I say is true is true. However, when it comes to the word of God, there is no my opinion vs. your opinion. Truth is only found in God.

Take a moment and ask yourself the hard questions.

- What lies have I believed about God's Word based on my emotions?
- What truth have I found myself believing that is actually a lie?

I recently saw the movie **Sound of Freedom**, and as I sat with a large butter popcorn on my lap, I casually ate bite after bite as the previews rolled. (Also, why can't we just pop one or two pieces into our mouth? Like seriously, I cram seven to ten pieces in my mouth with every bite. Okay, back to my story.) Y'all, as the movie began, I couldn't take another bite of popcorn. I passed the bucket to my husband, and I sat up in my chair with my elbows on my knees, leaning my body toward the screen. I felt compassion and an ache in my soul as the story unfolded, but I also felt a deep sense of conviction, and here is why. Human trafficking brings in so much money. I know it, and I have worked with girls who have been trafficked. I have seen with my own eyes the effects and trauma that it played on each of them. My heart has been broken for them in ways that kept me awake at night, begging God to use me just to

By Guarding What You've Been Given

do something. Is human trafficking real? 100% yes. But the conviction I felt for allowing myself to no longer talk about it genuinely made me feel repentant. It's one of those out-of-sight, out-of-mind things, and just because I am not directly involved in an organization or working with victims in this season, it doesn't take away from the truth of it all. I haven't even prayed about it in so long, y'all. I allowed my life circumstances, unsteady seasons with Richard's health, and ministry ups and downs to keep me from a fire burning in me for girls enslaved to the trauma of human trafficking no longer bother me. OUCH.

But if you step back and look at the big picture, we often treat it the same way regarding God's Word. We know God has called us to holiness, but our life circumstances and those desires that keep stirring within us push us to blur the lines just enough that we no longer run to God for direction, peace, clarity, or satisfaction. We allow ourselves to be swallowed up with our personal agendas, which does nothing to proclaim truth in our circles of influence because we often push God's Word to the back seat. We pick it up on Sundays and sometimes throughout the week when we scroll through a touching Instagram post with scripture attached, or sometimes we may seek prayer when we seem desperate for change. None of those things are bad by any means, but when you are only seeking God in the valleys or the darkness or only choosing to praise Him when things are going well, it shifts your view of God's Word, and ultimately, it affects how we walk in His truth.

On one of my trips to Honduras, I will never forget a conversation that my sweet friend and I had on the way to our ministry site. It was her first mission trip to another country. She asked me a question that now, looking back, I would have answered differently.

She asked me if I saw her as mature. I immediately responded with yes and listed a few reasons I believe that to be true.

However, it's not because of her circumstances or even her age. Honestly, I have seen her dig into God's Word; out of that, her depth and desire to walk in God's Word are so evident. Every conversation with her, she takes it back to Jesus. So yes, she is mature, but it's more than that. She is growing in the truth of God's Word, and out of that maturity, her faith is blooming.

God's Word is the game changer in every relationship, season change, prayer life, circumstance, deep valley moment, and mountain praise moment. Yes, it shifts our perspectives, and yes, it brings words that wash over our souls with healing, newness, and life change, but sweet friend, God's word is the foundation by which we have to choose to live our lives in EVERYthing we do. We will respond out of that depth, but also the lack thereof. Every time I begin to mentor a girl or woman, my question to them is, "Tell me what you have been reading in God's Word." I start with that question because it gives me insight into where they have been in their mind. It tells me that the weight of their circumstances probably feels so heavy or that their numbness directly correlates to not staying connected to the source of truth. It shows me where God's Word is on their priority list, and that alone says so much about the condition of their hearts. The moment we lean in the opposite direction of truth, we shift toward lies. Lies that seem normal and comfortable, ones that tell us scrolling on social media is more important than reading our Bible. The lies fog our minds with fear of provision because we see red in our bank accounts, yet we never go to God's Word about it. This is not me pointing my finger at you with a disappointed look. This is me leaning across the table, with my delicious latte I am sure, with tears in my eyes. I have been there, and I just desperately want you to understand God's Word is the ONLY source of truth that can and will move you, redeem you, and set you in the motion of walking in FREEDOM.

The moment we gave our lives to Him, God placed within us the Holy Spirit and this inner cry to need, want, and desire for His presence.

By Guarding What You've Been Given

For you did not receive the spirit of slavery to fall back into fear, but you have received the Spirit of adoption as sons, by whom we cry, "Abba! Father!"
Romans 8:15, ESV

I never want this book to stir up guilt in you. That's from the enemy, and I am not here for that. I am, however, here to encourage you to see things differently. I want you to not only read God's Word; I want you to embrace it with your whole heart. Our lives often look a lot like a see-saw in motion. We go from up to down with one swift push away from God's Word. It takes us to a place where we don't know how to get a steady footing. The days when you feel like you're on an emotional seesaw, when your breath gets knocked out of you because of words spoken to you, or abuse that happened to you, or the doctor's results that come in with zero hope. It's easy to sway in the direction of chaos and, by the world's standards, fear. But oh my goodness, when your heart has Jesus on the throne, the Holy Spirit shifts you with such a gentle nudge so you can feel your feet becoming steadfast in God's Word, His provision, His healing, and so on.

As we get closer to the end of this book, I want you to understand two things.

1. God's Word is true.
2. God's Word is the only truth.

We can fight to protect things like our hearts, our minds, our time, and even our callings, but if we aren't careful, we will crumble to whatever the enemy throws your way if we aren't fighting him with the only thing that will win this battle on this side of heaven: and that is the sword of truth.

Take a few minutes today and ask yourself a few hard questions.

Ask things like:

- What moved in the way of my time with Jesus lately?
- Who can I get to hold me accountable to seek God through His Word?
- What lies do I believe about God's Word or myself?

If we stay in a place of fog regarding what we believe, the fog will soon start clouding up the hard truths that are clearly in God's Word. It causes doubt, and then our judgment gets distorted.

Stay seeking God amid those days when unbelief whispers the lies, or you can't see the hand of God. Your faith is strengthened in those moments, and the fog begins to lift. If any chapter of this book needs to be written across your heart, it is this one because truth is the foundation on which every action is built. Your friendships, relationships, and all the daily activities are attached to your beliefs.

If you are in a place of doubt, please seek someone out. But also seek God for the answers you need and wait for Him.

CHAPTER 7

unBEARable:
"too painful or unpleasant for you to continue to experience"[11]

Have you ever felt the weight of something that seemed too painful or far too unpleasant? The pain that your body felt deep in your bones? I can point back to a few moments that felt like that and truly felt unbearable. When I think about it, it was when I stopped trying to carry the weight that it shifted inside my heart and mind. Did I feel the ache still? Absolutely, but allowing God to carry it through my worship and intentional leaning into Him relieved my weary soul.

It was a crisp August morning. It was not yet scorchingly hot and not cold enough for a sweatshirt. I sat on my back porch with my protein shake, coffee, and water bottle because, let's be honest, I have to have at least three beverages. I gathered my Bible, devotional book, and notebook, and as I sat down, I noticed that I had left my phone inside. I proceeded with my time with Jesus. I sat there in the stillness of an early morning and just listened. I listened to nature, I listened to the buzzing bees, I saw a hummingbird, I saw a sweet cardinal gathering twigs for a nest, and I felt calm take over my mind and soul. I began to pray for people, for things, for forgiveness, and for God to move boldly in some areas I had been begging Him to move in. I opened my Bible, and it was as if the words were screaming at me. I couldn't write fast enough. I remember waking over an hour and a half later, feeling full of God's presence. I truly felt so seen by Him and ready for my day. I repeated all the above a few days later, but I grabbed my phone this time. I sat down, and this time, I did have a sweatshirt on because it was a little chilly. I sat back and began to scroll. I responded to texts, sent funny memes to my friends, looked at my bank account, and felt anxious when I opened my Bible to start my time with God.

The only difference, besides the weather and my coffee flavoring, was my intentionality in being still and open to hearing God's voice, allowing the world to fill my head with screaming comparisons, lackings, and so on. The unbearable seasons that spring up out of our disobedience are the moments that can cause us to let our guard down.

I often find myself going back to the story of Ehud when I think about protecting what you cherish by guarding what you have been given. I get so frustrated with myself when it comes to laziness with my time management, or not seeing the scale move fast enough, or when ministry is hard (unbearable). I find myself wanting to lash out and then give up. *But God, in His goodness, reminds me that my obedience, paired with my surrender, does something in me.* It not only allows God to do mighty things in my life that bring Him glory. He uses the unbearable moments and the good, bad, and ugly and stands in the gap when I can't stand. He also reminds me that my surrender starts with my view of Him.

For example, Ehud was steadfast and loyal to God above all else. His act of obedience to kill the king had nothing to do with himself but everything to do with the call God had placed on His life. God raised Ehud, and he believed God wholeheartedly.

> *Then the people of Israel cried out to the LORD, and the LORD raised up for them a deliverer, Ehud, the son of Gera, the Benjaminite, a left-handed man.*
> Judges 3:15, ESV

God's Word reveals to us so much about His character. When

By Guarding What You've Been Given

we see God's character and learn who He is, the truth opens our eyes to see Him through the lens of more than a chore to check off. I went through the names of God, and afterward, I found myself praying strategically. I prayed to Jehovah Rapha when I needed healing. I prayed to Jehovah Jirah when I couldn't see the provision. His character never changes, and we see following Jesus as modifying our behaviors; we tend to become stagnant and self-reliant rather than allowing God's Word to transform us from the inside out. When we rely on God's Word, we rely on God alone to do the changing within us. I have read through many verses and passages of scripture over my life for the sole purpose of making me feel good, not change me. I leaned into the words that felt pretty and powerful yet didn't allow the truth of the Word to actually shift, remove, and renew what God was trying to change in me. If we are going to say we want God to move in our lives, even in those unbearable seasons, we have to actually respond when He shows us what our next step is to take, even if that means moving away from something or towards something that scares you out of your mind.

Throughout this book, we have discussed the importance of stepping into a place and allowing God to take the throne of your heart so you can see people, yourself, and the things you feel called to do from a different place. I allowed the very voice of people to keep me from walking in my calling for a few weeks (you want to talk about unbearable). It was unbearable because my heart and mind were in direct conflict. I wanted to believe those words, but I knew that God's Word deep inside me wouldn't let me. He began to show up in the sweetest ways and then confirmed it with His Word. You and I cannot change the world, but we can position ourselves and allow God to change us so that wherever we go, or whoever is in front of us sees Jesus, then we leave the life change to Him. All my life, I have heard people say things like, "Be careful how you live because you are a walking billboard for Jesus." If I am honest,

Protect What You Cherish

I have no idea what that means because billboards do not, in fact, walk, but I do understand that everything I do or don't do directly reflects how much I believe, trust, and follow Jesus. One of the things I have learned about myself over the last year or so is that I struggled with deep-rooted fear in me. I get scared often, and sometimes, (actually, every time), I feel fear begin to rise in me; I want to retreat to something that feels safe. For years, safety equated to food for me. I would use food as a means of protection. And in that place, I would be isolated even though people surrounded me.

Isolation is a tool the enemy uses to get us "feeling" alone so he can shame us into thinking what we are feeling is too big to handle. The reality is that sometimes it is too big because that's why fear sets in, and that is why we need to bring Jesus in before we ever get to the point of being paralyzed in fear.

In 2 Chronicles chapter 20, Jehoshaphat received word that a multitude was coming for him. It says in verse two:

Some men came and told Jehoshaphat, "a great multitude is coming against you from Eden, from beyond the sea; and behold they are in Hazazontamar"
2 Chronicles 20:2, ESV

He was afraid, yet his response was to seek the Lord.

Then Jehoshaphat was afraid and set his face to seek the Lord and proclaimed a fast throughout all Judah.
2 Chronicles 20:3, ESV

I think we get caught up in the response of fear and all that could happen, and we forget that God already knows everything and He isn't worried.

I have a new love for true crime shows and the police scanner.

By Guarding What You've Been Given

Y'all, I truly believe, at times, that I was meant to be a detective because I get so excited when I hear those alerts. I want to show at the crime scenes and help out, but I also know I can be the biggest chicken on the planet when it comes down to it. The truth is, I haven't always loved true crime shows. When I was little, I would never watch anything remotely scary before bed or any other time, for that matter. I hated haunted houses or anything that would taunt me when my lights went off at night. As an adult, I have always wanted a small light on "for protection." In my mind, I thought if I could see someone enter my room, I could at least be ready to fight. The other thought is that scary things lurk in the darkness, not the light. As I reflect on so many sleepless nights of waking up scared from random noise, to lying in my bed barely peeking over the covers, afraid of what I might see; goodness, so much has changed over the last few years. Truly, the dots are being connected, and I am sitting here with tears. (I am officially a crybaby). But somewhere along the way, I stopped being afraid of the dark. I believe with my whole heart God has given me a new confidence in His presence. Even as I finish this book, I can think back over seasons of fear that I allowed to creep into my mind and eventually slow me down in action and my calling. I kept my eyes off Jesus and onto myself. I looked at others and saw how well they were doing and how "badly" I seemed to be doing, and I would just stop praying for God to work in me.

If we aren't careful, we can make everything about us. Like Jehoshaphat, he could have easily responded in a way that would have given him protection. He was, however, more worried about seeking God, and that revealed what he held close.

How we respond in fear reveals what we hold near and dear and close to our hearts. For many of us, it's an appearance of looking as if you have it together. You end up making yourself so busy protecting what you want others to think versus what God has gifted YOU with. Your mind works the way it does because God created it that way.

I am not creative, and no matter how badly I try, I will forever be a contender for the show **Nailed It** over the show *Cupcake Wars*. I am the girl who will forever have a creative friend to create something for me, or I will buy it off Etsy, and I am okay with that. I remember showing up at family functions and friend gatherings feeling "less than" because I didn't bake some elaborate dish until I realized that was not me. I am so mad at myself for allowing those moments to define me. Did they shape me? YES, but that's it. But that's not me; I am 100% okay with it. If I have to, I will ask someone to make it for me, or I will gladly get a cute gift because that's my love language. I will meet with you one-on-one and give you all my attention, and I will jump on a plane today or tomorrow and go for a fun adventure. I am just sad it took me so long to embrace me. I was asked recently what I wanted the reader to get from my book, and it has changed over the last few years. It used to be I wanted you to pick up this book and feel empowered. I wanted you to see the people around you with new eyes and also see yourself differently. I still want you to do those things, but it's much more.

I want you to realize that where you are right now isn't by mistake.

I want you to know you have been given tools and truths to keep going and fight against the darkness, trying to snuff out that stirring dream or calling you're so afraid to step into. Those tools are tucked away in God's Word. His Word will help shape your thoughts, remove the clutter, and steady your feet when the unbearable seasons come your way.

By His divine power, God has given us everything we need for living a godly life. We have received all of this by coming to know Him, the one who called us to Himself by

By Guarding What You've Been Given

means of his marvelous glory and excellence.
2 Peter 1:3, NLT

I want you to know you can have peace and healthy relationships, walk confidently in freedom, and do mighty things in His name, even if that means you're single, heartbroken, waiting on God, or deep in a valley. God is never shocked by any of those things, and when we wrap our minds around the power attached to our surrender, something new begins to happen.

Like Ehud, we step with boldness, not fear. Maybe you feel fear, but it doesn't stop you; it propels you because you know Who is with you.

Therefore go and make disciples of all nations, baptizing them in the name of the Father and of the Son and of the Holy Spirit and teaching them to obey everything I have commanded you. And surely I am with you always, to the very end of the age.
Matthew 28:19-20, NIV

A fun fact about me is I am very competitive.

Ok, let me clarify. If I play a game of any kind, regardless if it's a card game, a trivia game, or something like musical chairs, you better believe I am all in, and I may or may not cheat, and I may or may not fight until the end so I can win. Once, I was at a fall retreat with students, and a game that entailed fighting for chairs in the dark was happening. And because I am competitive, I had to play. I left that game with a broken toe and also a victory, because I was for sure the last one standing (well, limping). If I do say so myself, the pain from that toe was unbearable (see what I did there). I have had broken ankles and two c-sections, and that broken toe was a doozy; ya'll it caused me to limp because of the pain literally. I was constantly afraid someone was going to step on it, or I was going to hit it on something until it healed.

The more I think about what the word "unbearable" means, the more I am reminded of the state in which Israel found itself before Ehud was on the scene. Let's review:

> *And the people of Israel served Eglon the king of Moab eighteen years. Then the people of Israel cried out to the Lord, and the Lord raised up for them a deliverer, Ehud, the son of Gera, the Benjaminite, a left-handed man. The people of Israel sent tribute by him to Eglon the king of Moab.*
> Judges 3:14-15

For eighteen long years, they served under an evil king, and I can almost hear the cries of the people. This place of desperation, fear, and hopelessness because of how unbearable (too painful and unpleasant) their season was. We think of seasons as a few months, or sometimes a year or two, but can you imagine eighteen long-suffering years of being under the authority of someone who didn't love God and mistreated them over and over. This book has reminded me more than you know of the seasons I deemed unbearable because of heartache, betrayal, or consequences of my own words or disobedience. The only theme that has played out has been those "crying out" moments where I begged God to change my season. While, in all reality, He was changing my season, He was also changing me amid those hard seasons. I have learned what true, genuine friendship is now, and I never want to return. I have learned my body needs to be protected and guarded at all costs because it matters when it comes to the things I feel called to do. I have learned the Bible is more than a book; it reflects God's heart, and every word is true regardless of what the world (or TikTok) proclaims. I have learned my calling is not your calling, and it's up to me to take each step in surrender and believe if God called me to it, He will give me exactly what I need to follow through and do it.

By Guarding What You've Been Given

I have learned the body of Christ is essential in my life. The world bashes the church a lot, and I have experienced people within churches that have crushed my soul in seasons, and I am sure my words have hurt others too, but the body of Christ is beautiful and has truly become one of my greatest joys. I have learned peace isn't something that you feel. It's something that Jesus is. He is my peace amid dark storms, sleepless nights, or dancing on the mountaintops. He is peace, and regardless of the battle you and I will face, peace is attainable because Jesus never leaves our side. He promises us that he will walk with us.

Let's look back at our friend Ehud once again. How much goodness is packed into those verses in Judges 3:12-30 blows my mind.

Right after the Israelites cried out to God, it says Ehud was raised. So that means more waiting was happening. Even more painful days of being under the authority of King Moab. He was evil, and although God raised Ehud, he didn't slay the king when he was a toddler. Unbearable seasons will push us either deeper into God's strength and power or cause us to run deeper into a place of desperation. Ehud was being raised in the same season as King Moab's reign, yet Ehud was loyal to the Lord. I love verse 16.

And Ehud made for himself a sword with two edges, a cubit in length, and he bound it on his right thigh under his clothes.
Judges 3:16, ESV

Let's press pause on verse 16. Ehud was left-handed, and every weapon around him was tailored for the right-handed soldier. Ehud didn't question why he was left-handed. Instead, he made a sword for himself that he could use. I am embarrassed at how many times I have complained about my height, body shape, or intelligence level. I honestly have complained or even questioned more times than I can count about why God wired me or designed me in such a way. The more I walk in His freedom, the more I see clearly that He intended to use it for His glory. The seasons of disobedience started with me complaining about it, hiding behind it, crying for God to change it. But my goodness, what if I had seen its beauty and allowed God to use it without hesitation? I will never know what could have happened, but now I refuse to let the enemy to taunt me with the "what ifs." God not only raised Ehud, but He also gave him precisely what he needed for the moment he would meet the king face to face. In all the years of equipping Ehud as a left-hand warrior, it was also in the hidden places that a sword was created for Him. He waited for one of those divine appointments. You know, the ones that you just can't seem to shake because you know it's a God appointment. A "for such a time as this moment." Just like He raised Ehud, He is also raising you with specific quirks and giftings to use for His glory right where you are and in the battles ahead.

Truthfully, the world wants our gifts to reflect who we are so that it brings us glory, while God gifts us with the very things we often complain about. He wants us to follow Him wholeheartedly and then surrender everything we have so that when we step out and do the things He has called us to, it will always go back to Him and never ourselves.

Could you imagine if we read about Ehud trying to get through the king's quarters with a right-handed weapon? He wouldn't have gotten through with such ease. There would have been a bloody battle, for sure. Instead, he made a weapon tailored to his design for himself. Your calling, time, peace, relationships, friendships, and giftings have been given to you so that you confidently walk boldly into places and seasons. Not because of anything you will do or have done but because you chose to "make for yourself" weapons that represent the power of God in you. The way you write, the way you speak, the way you love people, and the way you work and do things from day to day

By Guarding What You've Been Given

are sweet glimpses of Christ in you, the hope of Glory. Don't hide those things. Instead, pull them out and guard what you have been given, because the world needs to see God at work.

> *24 Now I rejoice in my sufferings for your sake, and in my flesh I am filling up what is lacking in Christ's afflictions for the sake of his body, that is, the church, 25 of which I became a minister according to the stewardship from God that was given to me for you, to make the word of God fully known, 26 the mystery hidden for ages and generations but now revealed to his saints. 27 To them God chose to make known how great among the Gentiles are the riches of the glory of this mystery, which is Christ in you, the hope of glory. 28 Him we proclaim, warning everyone and teaching everyone with all wisdom, that we may present everyone mature in Christ. 29 For this I toil, struggling with all his energy that he powerfully works within me.*
> Colossians 1:24-29, ESV

For most of my life, I have struggled with the same things. They would disguise themselves in different ways or pop up at times that I least expected, but looking back on even my childhood, the struggles seemed so big and unbearable. I don't remember anyone ever speaking about those struggles, but honestly, I covered them up and never really allowed anyone close to my heart.

Many of you are sitting in your college dorm rooms fighting against the same thoughts you had as a middle school girl, or maybe even as a small little girl, and you are so over it. You have begged God to remove the narrative you have allowed to be etched into your brain. Thoughts like you will never see God move in _____ (you fill in the blank), or feelings of never seeing God bring you the desires of your heart. I am so sorry for the young, newly married woman whose heart has been crushed by betrayal and who feels so distant from your spouse. I am sorry to the teen girl who passes through the halls of her school with fear of being either seen and made fun of or unseen and rejected. Maybe the issue isn't YOU. Maybe, just maybe, God hand-crafted you to be where you are right now, and He has a much better and bigger plan, and you just need to shift your perspective.

I remember when my stepdad came into my life when I was in the ninth grade. I was BOY CRAZY, to say the least. He stepped in with such strict rules, and I was shocked. I couldn't call boys, they had to call me. I couldn't listen to music before bed because I needed to let my mind rest. I couldn't stay out late because there was no reason to be out when most things were closed. I rebelled in words and sometimes actions, and I got grounded and my keys taken (and my landline phone in my room removed), but those quickly became the moments I look back to that began to shift my whole perspective of how I see my worth. He pushed hard, and now I speak about worthiness in girls' lives. I just had to see things from a different perspective.

Let today be the day you begin no longer seeing yourself through the lens of your size, past, or even the places you feel you're lacking. Instead, start seeing God for who He is, and allow Him to guard your mind with His Word. His Word will bring about this beautiful transformation and take you from what you don't have to Whom you belong. *In Him, you will find satisfaction, peace in the weary seasons, hope amid deep dark seasons, and joy for the journey along the way.*

Please press pause for a moment. Pray and ask God to give you someone you can reach out to and share with them where you feel insecure or fearful, and ask them to hold you accountable in choosing to believe truth over lies. Accountability isn't judgment. It is not to hurt you but instead to help you. I also challenge you to gather some scriptures to help you with the lies you're currently believing. I am not saying you don't feel some hard things, nor am I invalidating the spaces of wounds that others have given to you. Those things are hard to navigate through, and I know that insecurities are real and can be crippling if we allow them to be. But, oh, sweet friend, when you get a hold of the truth that every insecurity is rooted in a lie, it intentionally changes the trajectory of what we dwell on. Bring someone into that place and allow those words to speak life over your mind and soul. Also, while you're on pause, seriously, grab some Post-it notes (I am serious when I say Post-it notes should sponsor me. I have them in my Bible, on my mirrors, on the microwave, and anywhere I need to be reminded of the truth.) Write out some scriptures that speak directly to the areas you find yourself limping—the places where these unbearable emotions that keep you from walking in your calling keep tripping you up. Speak into those things with the only words that can break the chains and snap those weapons from the enemy into pieces.

It is time you speak truth into the darkness, friend, because the enemy will run. He can't stand in the presence of our Holy God. He hates anything that leans in the direction of what is holy.

For you have delivered my soul from death, yes my feet from falling that I may walk before God in the light of life.
Psalm 56:13, ESV

He delivered me from those things so I may walk in the light. That means every step, every word, and every thought gets filtered through the light. Once the light shines on it, God exposes the darkness, and it's up to me to run in the opposite direction. We don't need to stand around on slippery slopes when we can have a firm footing in the power of God to redeem us and set us free. I don't know if you're like me, but walking up any hill takes the breath out of me. I have walked up many hills in Haiti and Honduras, and both had me panting and unable to talk because I couldn't catch my breath. As I think about one of those hills, particularly in Honduras, I am reminded of when I fell down a hill (it felt like a mountain). I lost my footing because my eyes were focused on the magnitude of the hill and not the step in front of me. When I fell, my feet began slipping. My balance left me, and both knees went into the rocks and gravel that made up this hill (that seemed like a ginormous mountain). First came the stinging, then the blood, and then the flies swarming. My friend came to rescue me with something to clean it, and everything in me wanted to hit her right in the face because of how bad it hurt. The cleaning was part of keeping that wound from getting infected. I could have easily slapped on a bandaid and gone on about my business, but the wound would have only been covered, not cleaned. For most of us, we do that often in our everyday lives. We cover up the wounds by dressing them with spending money, eating, or running from one relationship to the next. We allow the hole of emptiness to grow simply because we refuse to deal with the core of it all. Whether it's a sin issue on your end and the consequences seem too hard to deal with or the sin and consequences of someone else, both are hard things to recover from.

Think about the Olympic games, for example. Those athletes fall often, get hurt, forget their routines, and sometimes just have a slow day. Does that mean they just need to leave that sport and give up on their dreams of being a medalist? Absolutely not. Instead, it's a reminder that there is still work to be done and room for growth. If you have ever quit something prematurely and know the regret you feel when it finally sets in, then you know what I am talking about. Sometimes, God calls us away from things because it's time to shut the door on that season. Sometimes, our knee-jerk reaction to not getting our way causes us to shut the door too soon. I don't want that for you, friend. I want you to understand that holy things come in hard and sometimes unbearable (see what I did there again) seasons. The hard thing is shaping you, not to be perfect, but to embrace the holiness of God through something called sanctification. I know it's a "churchy" word, but it's a word that brings so much weight to how holiness works in my mind.

By Guarding What You've Been Given

The theological definition of sanctification of someone or something is to set that person or thing apart for the use intended by its designer.[12]

Y'all, that is SO good. God, in all His holiness, chooses to set you and me apart for an intended purpose. HE CHOSE YOU and ME right where we are, not where we want or even ought to be. That gets me so fired up. You're not a mistake, and you are meant to be the mom, wife, sister, friend, teacher, missionary, in a season of waiting, employee, or student right now in this very season. The beauty of sanctification is hard, but oh so holy. I have a picture of Jesus not standing over me or at a distance but instead up close. As He looks me in my eyes, He already knows every anxious thought, every struggle, and every choice I have and will make, and He still chooses me. He leans a little closer, and one by one, He pours out His truth, and it begins to wash over my heart, mind, and life. One by one, He removes the sins, the shame, and the fears because those things can't stand in the presence of His holiness. That picture is sanctification. Does it hurt? Sometimes, but not because Jesus is mean. It's because He is kind.

> *Or do you show contempt for the riches of his kindness, forbearance and patience, not realizing that God's kindness is intended to lead you to repentance?*
> Romans 2:4, NIV

Repentance was never meant to make you feel bad about yourself. I think that word has somehow turned into a concept we must keep our hearts away from because it somehow messes with our peace. When, in fact, peace follows repentance because it sets us back in the direction of holiness. You and I will never be perfect, and I know I have said that already, but sometimes, we need to hear something more than once to let it settle in our hearts.

Have you ever wanted something so badly that you thought

about it a lot? Of course, you have. I bet if you and I could have a coffee date, and I asked you things like:

Your favorite restaurant? Your favorite gift as a child? Your favorite TV show? I bet you could tell me the details surrounding each one—things like what you order at your favorite restaurant. I bet you could tell me your favorite childhood gift and what made it special. I bet you could tell me not only about your favorite TV show but also the exact episode you love or what about it brings you back over and over.

For example, my husband loves two shows, **The Office** and **Seinfeld**. He has seen every episode but sometimes wants to watch a specific one. It's one he laughs at every single time. It's not necessarily nostalgic as much as it is comfort. His brain doesn't have to invest too much because he knows what will happen. Once, he lost vision in both eyes, and it was a hard few weeks. However, every time we sat down to watch TV, he would request a specific episode from one of those shows, simply because he didn't need to see it to see it in his mind.

What if we approached God's Word and God himself like this? What if we get so comfortable trusting God to show up even when we can't see what's happening? What if we get so confident in the ending because we know God always has our best interest in mind? We know the ending is not our ending because we get an eternity to love and soak up His presence without an ounce of wondering or wandering ever again. I don't know about you, but that greatly encourages my heart. Being able to look ahead with my hands open is somewhere I desire to be in all seasons, no matter what. But you and I must be disciplined to come to God with daily repentance—not this idea that you have to be good at praying and asking for forgiveness, but instead, a heart posture of knowing you have sinned against a Holy God, and through that repentance, we are made right with Him so we can no longer walk in the comfort of wandering off.

By Guarding What You've Been Given

Protecting what you cherish by guarding what you have been given was born out of so much heartache, discipline, and burning away of a lot of self. But I am so thankful for the deep valley, "seemingly unbearable" moments because the small steps of obedience, repentance, and surrender led me to see God and myself through a new lens. This is what I pray for you, too, before you start the last chapter . . .

(Wait, did I just say the last chapter? WOW.)

(Okay, sorry, that was a teary moment for me.)

Before you start the last chapter, I want you to press pause once again. Use the next page as a prayer of surrender. There is something about getting our prayers onto paper. Even if you burn that paper or throw it in the trash, go ahead and write it all out because He already knows it all. He wants to meet you exactly where you are, so go ahead and let Him in.

Protect What You Cherish

By Guarding What You've Been Given

CHAPTER 8

The LORD makes firm the steps of the one who delights in him; though he may stumble, he will not fall, for the LORD upholds him with his hand.
Psalm 37:23-24, NIV

Moving Day

Have you ever purchased anything on the internet without reading the reviews? If you answered yes, then we would be friends. However, I am now becoming the person who reads the reviews. I suddenly started reading the reviews when I received a bag of clothes that were all too tight. On top of being unable to return the clothes, I also lost the money I spent on them. I would have known to size up if I had just read the reviews. I am the worst at reading the small print, and because I missed those details, I lost out on some cute clothes and money.

For many of you, loss has been a part of your story. Maybe death took away someone you loved deeply, or perhaps you lost someone through betrayal. Either way, the loss is a sting that hurts deeply. It causes you to second-guess a lot of things, including moving forward. We are coming to the close of this book, and goodness, I am so glad it's the end because it's been a tough few years of wrestling through every chapter. But I have experienced loss along the way, and even as I sit in this coffee shop, my heart still aches at times over it. The hard part is when you want to park it and no longer trust others after friendship loss, or park it in fear because you're afraid of what could happen to someone else you love in your life. But, once you finally start moving forward, fixing your eyes on what's in front of you can be challenging. In Psalm 37, David reminds us God himself holds us and helps us establish firm footing. When it becomes too hard to take that step forward, God makes our steps firm, and this verse reminds us that stumbling may (often) happen. The Lord upholds you and me with His hand on us. God revives dreams that once laid dormant, awakens the passion we let slip away, and moves us in a new direction of healing while restoring what was lost. It brings Glory to His name when we step in the direction of Jesus. I have realized the scars we have from broken relationships and friendships of the present or past are just reminders of healing. The scars also teach us how to do things differently. I approach my marriage and my friendships differently because of the scars I have from my past.

I only wrote one chapter on better friendships/relationships together, but I wanted to come back to that topic for a moment (I told you I would revisit this). Do you have those friends who can look at your face and know where you are emotionally? Ugh, I do, and sometimes I wish they couldn't read me so well. I figured out why they can. It is because they chose to stay, even when it wasn't easy. In fact, on days when I reach out for prayer, it blows my mind how quickly they run to carry me in prayer and lavish me in God's word. The thing about these particular friendships is that each of them started in different places and seasons of my life. Some came from me mentoring them; others came from a place of loneliness and me begging God for deep friendships. There is something so sweet that God does when He's the one who weaves together his daughters' hearts. I cherish those friends so much.

But, when I think about Ehud, I don't see anything about his close friends carrying him in prayer, nor do I hear about his friends standing with him in the king's quarters. For most of my life, I was dependent on the approval of others to the point it was immobilizing. I have even allowed those close friends

By Guarding What You've Been Given

to bring me worth in some seasons. God's Word has shown me that it's not friendship that moves mountains; it is God. If we aren't careful, we begin to nurture and protect the wrong things. Please do not hear me say that you don't need to nurture and guard your friendships (I wrote an entire chapter on it). However, when anything stands in the way of following Jesus wholeheartedly, it's an idol, whether you believe that or not. We guard the things that make us feel safe. Yes, even friendships, approval, that job, that relationship. Even those feelings of rejection and loss can quickly become the very thing you guard with your life and nurture because it feels like you're normal. Anything outside of those emotions makes you feel out of control, and before you know it, you fight to keep those things intact.

It hurts my heart to think about all the unhealthy habits, thought patterns, friendships, relationships, and secret sins over the years that caused me to miss God moving because I chose to be stuck behind, protecting and defending the wrong thing. I nurtured what the enemy set out to derail me with. The enemy's ploy to keep us isolated and lonely has driven a new passion in me to pursue peace, see people, and truly open my heart up for new depths in friendships. It's easy to be alone and shut people out. I get it. Really, I do. I have scars that date back to kindergarten and scars from middle school and high school. I have scars that remind me of ministry days of crying myself to sleep because of the hurt I felt. I have reached out to people begging for conversations, and nothing has been returned, which immediately felt like rejection. Now, stepping back, I see so much protection over my heart and mind. The friendships that have come into my life and my current friendships allow me to see grace through a different lens. I want hard conversations, and I want others to see me for me, but I also want to see them, hear them, and truly meet them where they are without any expectation attached to it. I am sure my words have caused scars, and I am sure some of my actions have, too, but in the end, I can only let go of that regret and try to pursue peace and allow God to either reconcile it or allow me (and them) to walk away from it without bitterness. So, sweet friend, if that is you in this season, with hurt, anger, resentment, or feeling like that wound will never heal and become a scar, hear me say, wounds eventually scab over. Some wounds heal without a trace, and some leave a scar as a reminder of the wreckage. It is time to lean into God's Word and allow His Word to salve those wounds. You and I are worthy of Biblical community and deep friendships, and I will never believe anything else.

Gracious words are a honeycomb, sweet to the soul and healing to the bones.
Psalm 16:24, ESV

Let that sit for a few minutes. I know I chased the friendship squirrel into this chapter, but I needed to press down once again. If this is for you, stop and take a moment to pray for those who have deeply wounded your heart. Ask God for forgiveness for things you have said or done to someone else. It is so important to say what we mean and then mean what we say. A few years ago, we were on the road to Santa Rosa, Florida, with some friends. Brad is one of the funniest people I have ever known. He can preach the house down, lead worship, and make me laugh until I can't breathe. This was one of those trips. It was after a Sunday, and Brad, Ariel, Richard, and I were tired from church but excited to start our vacation. However, Richard was hungry, and we were in an unfamiliar place. Richard began telling Siri to take us to Magic Mike's. Now, he meant Jersey Mike's, which sells subs. But every time Siri didn't understand, he just yelled it louder. I am not kidding when I couldn't breathe from laughing—one, because of Richard's miscommunication, and, two, Brad's commentary from the backseat.

He didn't actually say what he meant.

By Guarding What You've Been Given

I am here to tell you that healing is coming, friend ... I believe it for you because I have experienced that same healing.

A few years ago, I was coming out of bondage while also seeing a lot of new areas of my heart that were very much still attached to old ways of thinking or habits that continually had me in chains. It wasn't until I allowed those areas to be exposed that God began to transform me from the inside out. The lies I believed about myself or others were the foundations on which I built my friendships. It makes me cringe thinking about how much I let things get by me, whether it was intentional conversations that left me feeling defeated or words I said just to fit in. But freedom has taken the blind spots and brought them directly in front of me, and it has been the most beautiful thing and has transformed my current friendships.

Blind spots get me sometimes when I am driving on the interstate. It's partially because I drive a Honda Pilot, and it's bigger, so smaller cars will sneak up on me, and I almost run them off the road when I try to change lanes. I will take a quick glance because if I stare in the opposite direction, I could cause a crash. So I keep my eyes on what's in front of me while checking my side mirrors constantly, with a glance here and there for potential threats coming into my lane.

Looking back can cause us to miss what's in front of us and no longer proclaim what God is doing right now. When I think about the word "proclaim," it reminds me I am setting my heart and mind on something. My words and actions reflect those things. Proclaiming means I can't look back to ponder where I have come from but instead what God did within me and where I am headed.

Don't look back.
This means you should not turn around and go in the opposite direction.

Proclaim the power of God, whose majesty is over Israel, whose power is in the heavens.
Psalm 68:34, ESV

I always tell people that everyone is one step away from sin. Good marriages can go bad with one lapse of judgment. Every teenage girl who has held on to her purity is one decision away from walking out of a bedroom in shame. Every dream birthed in us is one decision away from only becoming a thought. That one moment or that one decision are defining moments in our lives. If we know that God's redeeming love brings FREEDOM, why is it that we live as if we are still in bondage? I believe it is because the enemy knows that if he can keep us looking back at who we used to be, we won't fully embrace where God is taking us and all He has for us. We must choose Jesus in every moment and with every decision because the moment we lose sight of Him, fear will set in, and we will begin to proclaim a life that is not only led by fear but also disobedience.

Let's look at Psalm 68:34 again:

Proclaim the power of God, whose majesty is over Israel, whose power is in the heavens.

If we allow the stressors of this world to be what we choose to proclaim, what are we projecting about God? The God who spoke the world into existence and placed a baby in a virgin's belly wants to use your story, your season, and your voice to proclaim His power.

Look for moments to declare God's power and then live like you mean it because SOMEONE needs to see God's power alive in YOU! Sometimes, we become so impatient with wanting to see God move instantly that we stop proclaiming and start complaining instead.

By Guarding What You've Been Given

I would call myself a pretty patient person. I can sit in traffic and not get irritated. I can get behind the coupon lady in the store and not get frustrated, but I have become pretty impatient when waiting for God to move in an area. So, when it comes to proclaiming, let's dive deeper into the importance of waiting patiently.

Waiting patiently means responding obediently regardless of whether we see the outcome.

When I went to Thailand, I will never forget the stories told by one of the women I met. I cannot remember her name, but I will forever remember her standing up in the restaurant and sharing her personal story of finding Jesus in a country deeply committed to worshipping Buddha. She was beaten and pushed out of her family. She was brave and all in for Jesus. She also shared with us that when they started the Christian private school in Thailand, they could never see beyond just starting the school. They knew God had called them to teach English and share the gospel. They waited patiently and with such expectation, and now, years later, hundreds of kids have heard the gospel, and their ministry is growing.

This precious lady, who went from serving Buddah to serving Jesus, was beaten by her parents. Through the pain, she waited for God to move, trusting and worshipping him alone. She just knew she couldn't go back to worshiping Buddha.

When we were there, they were busy preparing for their upcoming Christmas program and expected over a thousand people to attend. Wow, right? In a country where less than 1% believe in Jesus, a couple who surrendered everything chose to stand firm, not bow to fear, and wait with their whole hearts for the fruit of their obedience.

In 1 Corinthians, Paul is writing to the church in Corinth. Chapter 3, verse 6 says:

Protect What You Cherish

I planted, Apollos watered but God gave the growth, so neither he which plants nor he who waters is anything but only God who gives growth (ESV).

That means when you boldly proclaim the name of Jesus, the results aren't up to you—ONLY GOD. Your marriage can be amazing simply by the words you choose to speak to your spouse and how you love them, and through your obedience, God will bring growth. Whatever season you are in, and no matter what it looks like, it's not up to you to get the outcome, but it is your responsibility to walk in obedience. God will use a season of brokenness that may result from your disobedience or someone else's because He is a God who makes all things new.

Over the last few years, my prayers have become fueled by surrender. I want my life to proclaim who God is and the love that He pours out so graciously over me. Be encouraged today to stand firm, no longer look back, and wait patiently because God has something in store for you and those who will look to you to see Him through you. Patience is hard. Every time I see those videos of little kids having to wait before their parents return to eat the dessert on their plates, it always makes me laugh but also teaches something so sweet to my soul. Sometimes, God says no, not because He withholds or punishes us but because He can see what's best for us. He may say not right now, or just wait a little longer, or He may blow your mind with something beyond your imagination. The problem comes when we focus on a timeline rather than Jesus. Our impatience escalates when things don't go our way, and we feel unseen or heard by God. Remember that patience isn't something you have to obtain; it was gifted to you through the Holy Spirit and your salvation. You have the muscle of peace; you just have to exercise it to walk in it. It's allowing the timelines to be thrown away and the plans attached to your desires to be set aside so that the plans of God and His way lead you into bigger and better things. His way will bring the most glory because God will be exalted through your stories, obedience, and surrender.

Finishing strong has been an issue for most of my life. I like doing fun things, and anything outside of that has felt like a chore. From writing this book to folding laundry to having hard conversations with people I never thought I would have, those all seem like weights that are just too heavy for my brain to carry. It wasn't until recently, as in the beginning of October 2023, that I was diagnosed with ADHD. I have been embarrassed to say it a couple of times, and that was only because I didn't want to hear things like "It's about time" or "Now you'll get it together." First of all, RUDE. I have definitely heard both of those. At first, I could feel lies bubbling up, but then I grabbed that lie and said nope, it was not getting anywhere near my heart. I sat in my doctor's office with tears streaming down my face, and as he talked and explained so much to me, all I could think of was that I wanted to do ministry strong, and I wanted to finish well so that those who are behind me are set up to lead stronger. I want the next generation to seek God, stand confident, walk in freedom, and speak boldly.

As I break down those things, it is the perfect way for me to encourage you as we finish this book.

Protecting what you cherish by guarding what you have been given. If you possess something in this current season, then God ordained it. But remember, it's not ours to own, so first surrender it and then be ready to protect it at all costs because the One who holds the authority over it will get you through it.

1. Seeking God

Are you reading your Bible daily? If not, start there. To seek the heart of God, you must seek Him through His Word. It's where you see God's character through a holiness lens. It sets you up to seek Him wholeheartedly. You fall in love with God over and over again while also seeing the sacredness of His Words passed down to us from the beginning of time. The Word of God is true. We have to start at that place within our hearts if we are going to walk in truth. His Word removes and exposes so that we can align our lives with His Word in the hope that we are no longer enslaved to lies. Bondage isn't normal, and as believers, we can't afford to live life as normal. There is truly nothing normal about following Jesus.

2. Stand confidently

Confidence is a word that most women don't attach themselves to yet, but they totally should. God's Word says this in Ephesians 3:12 (NIV):

In Him and through faith in Him, we may approach God with freedom and confidence.

Have you ever felt so sure of something that you approached whatever it was with confidence? I remember walking into a football stadium that was predominantly the other teams' fans. But because my team (Florida State Seminoles) had an undefeated record up to that point, I walked confidently past everyone wearing the opposing team. I walked with my shoulders back and with a little swag because I knew we were going to walk out of there victorious. The same goes for following Jesus. Regardless of your life or season, the end game is Jesus wins, which means you win, and in that comes a level of confidence that NO ONE can take from you. Go ahead, approach the throne room with your hands held high, your heart postured to hear from God, and then walk confidently in His steadfast love.

3. Walk in freedom

Freedom will always be a word that makes me feel all giddy

inside. I know that until I get to walk the streets of gold in Heaven and eat all the Oreos I want, declaring freedom and living out freedom is what I am called to do right now. Freedom is on the other side of everything that the enemy uses to enslave us, and I refuse to let him be the loudest voice in the lives of girls and women. Freedom is recognizing that even in loss, grief, and struggles that suffocate our passion or hardships that shipwreck our faith, we believe Jesus is fully who He says He is, and we are who He says we are, regardless of the wreckage in front of us or surrounding us. Wreckage isn't the end. FREEDOM IS because Jesus is.

Now, the Lord is the Spirit, and where the Spirit of the Lord is, there is freedom.
2 Corinthians 3:17, ESV

When we rest in the presence of Jesus, peace and freedom follow—freedom that cost Jesus His life yet gave us life to live to the fullest. Freedom is looking into the reflection of a window and no longer seeing the flaws but the reflection of God's beauty. Freedom reminds you it's not about your ability but God's power in you. Freedom is not something you have to beg God for or perform to receive. Instead, when you embrace Jesus, you get to walk in freedom. What's it going to take for you? Is it being real with yourself about the areas that you are continuing to walk in bondage in? Is it calling those out and bringing godly counsel in to help point you to scripture so that you can overcome those things? You were never meant to walk in failure. Freedom is owning up to things that keep you shrinking back and then choosing Jesus, receiving His grace, and walking in the direction of freedom over and over and over. I truly believe we have to choose to walk in freedom every single day. Are you ready to hear those chains hit the floor? Gosh, I can almost hear those insecurities clanging to the floor. Stop the enemy's weapons trajectory by allowing God's Word to break those arrows in half. For every chain link, there are new levels of God's grace and mercy, and I pray that you will no longer allow the enemy to taunt you. You have been given a beautiful purpose to protect, leading me to the last part: BOLDNESS.

4. Speak with boldness

Boldness is something we fear these days because we don't want to be canceled. So, I want to help you process this word from a different angle. I don't know about you, but stepping onto a roller coaster with huge drops, a few flips, and twists and turns always fills my stomach with butterflies. I love a good roller coaster, don't get me wrong, but I also have these thoughts almost every time I ride it:

Will the coaster come off the track? Will I fit on this ride? Will my seatbelt break in the middle of the ride? Will I get stuck in my seat, and will people have to watch me squirm out?

But as soon as I step on the ride and the first drop or twist comes, something happens; I no longer feel fear or excitement, and fearlessness bubbles up in me. I usually get off ready to ride again and want someone else to experience it with me. That, to me, is a beautiful picture of boldness. It's experiencing Jesus and never being able to shut up about Him. The things that have the potential to keep us quiet are the things that keep us enslaved to fear. The enemy wants you to keep your mouth shut because he knows the power of God. This, my friend, is our

"FOR SUCH A TIME AS THIS" MOMENT.

If you're holding this book and have made it to this page, I hope you feel something stirring. I hope you feel the power of God breathing new life over your ministry and heart. I hope you can feel the chains falling off the God-given things God has called you to. The next generation is counting on you and me to carry the Word of God into their generation while calling

By Guarding What You've Been Given

them up, not out. They need truth paired with grace. I need truth paired with grace. You need truth paired with grace. It is something every one of us needs, yet only Jesus is the one who pours it out over and over and over. Sin will always push you in a corner and silence you, because after he tempts you with sin, he throws shame and guilt your way until you wear it as if it was yours alone. I wish I could sit across from you right now and, one by one, remove the lies your heart keeps believing and your mind keeps running to. Boldness in Christ has nothing to do with how you were wired. It is the power of God in you.

For many people, boldness is attached to an extroverted personality type, and because so many people feel shy, they don't think there is boldness in them. Sometimes, boldness isn't about speaking louder; it's about choosing to speak at all. Boldness is not about doing things for people to see. Sometimes, it is about serving when no one else can see. Boldness is allowing your money, your time, your heart, your mind, your calling, and your relationships and friendships to be wrapped up in the goodness of God with no strings attached to an expectation. Boldness is paired with a holy expectancy of God, which is what only He can do. It's choosing to be used regardless of the how or even the why. It's saying I will boldly change the toilet paper in the bathroom stall, I will boldly buy that person groceries, or I will boldly stand on stage and use my gift of singing or teaching. Again, boldness is your bold moves of obedience attached to the power of God. Goodness, I don't know if that moves your soul, but I want my boldness to rise so that when the people in this world without hope look my way, I reflect Jesus.

As I bring this book to a close, I am forced to reflect on the wrestling matches between me and God over the last few years. The amount of awareness of my own personal sin, the weight of heartache, along with deep surrender, have brought me to this place almost five years later. I don't understand everything that has happened since 2020, but I know I wouldn't return. The pain pushed me deeper into intimacy with Jesus. The heartache and loss of friendships that I thought were forever have allowed me to see the importance of Biblical community along with understanding the reality that the enemy is always out to destroy it. I have to be honest, transparent with some, and vulnerable with many while pursuing peace over and over and over. For many of you, your words to keep going have kept my fingers on the keyboard. Your texts, coffee dates, and prayers pushed me when I truly wanted to quit this entire journey. But protecting what I cherish by guarding what I have been given has truly changed me. It has allowed me to see people differently but has also exposed so much inside me. I don't think I will ever get over the kindness of God. It says in Romans 2, it is "God's kindness that leads us to repentance." He doesn't point me to the cross, He doesn't drag me to the cross, and He doesn't turn his back while I crawl to the cross. No, the kindness of God leads me, carries me, and shows me the way of repentance so I can experience the fullness of who He is and who He has called me to be.

I mentioned earlier that I was recently diagnosed with ADHD, and it's something that, for most of my life, people have made little jokes here and there about me being "undiagnosed ADHD." I would laugh and agree, but it wasn't until I sat across from dinner with my friend Candace that tears filled my eyes, and I felt the disconnect in my brain as she explained so much about it. She knew the exhaustion my brain felt because she, too, has ADHD. It was the sweetest bond God cultivated that night. I came home and immediately scheduled a doctor's appointment for the following week. As I took the evaluation, I couldn't help but laugh (literally out loud) because every question I answered was "very often" or "often" (describes me). In fact, only two were "often," and the rest were "very often." After the doctor talked to me and helped me understand what medicine would do, I walked out hopeful, but if I am

By Guarding What You've Been Given

honest, I truly didn't understand how my brain could shift simply because of medicine. I took my first dose, and, to my amazement, suddenly, my brain was zoned in on one thing at a time. I finished sentences, and I made eye contact. I had my chores done by 9 a.m., and the amount of energy, relief, and thankfulness I felt was unmatched. I couldn't believe I had struggled this long in life. I can't even begin to tell you all of the anxious nights I have suffered with my mind racing that has then led me to feel so defeated over and over. I would second guess, chase a million squirrels in my mind and thoughts would spiral, all while I was dreaming big for Jesus. Sounds like torture, doesn't it? Even now, I feel focused and relaxed, and my brain has never chased a stupid rabbit (HAHA, but seriously). I would often sit down to write this book, have a thought or remember I hadn't done something, or find myself shopping on Amazon literally from one thought, y'all. I tell you all this because it has given me new insight into this call to protect what we cherish.

When I look back at the beginning, when I was just starting to write this book, I truly thought I was going to just talk about Ehud and how God used his left-handed uniqueness, paired with devotion and surrender, to bring peace for eighty years to the Israelites, because many of you so desperately need peace. But I have seen it from a different angle throughout the last few years. There were many things in the way for Ehud, yet he followed through, regardless of the potential threat that awaited him. Friend, your insecurities may have come from a lot of pain, maybe even from trauma or failures and mistakes over the years, but let me be clear, the enemy feeds you lie after lie about who you are and who you aren't so that he can STOP YOU. He wants nothing more than those insecurities to keep you from obeying God and block you by making those insecurities become bigger in your mind rather than believing the power of God in you.

Protect What You Cherish

They are lies. I can't stress that enough. Truth is not tucked away or will ever be tucked away in insecurities. If you are trapped in this spot, please go to God's Word (grab those Post-it notes, write the Word of God on them, and then put it all over your house).

It is time to let go once and for all of the bondage that has enslaved you thus far. The Word of God is your weapon, and it's time you use it to fight back. God wants to use you. He wants to use your stories, your weakness, and all the sweet valley and mountain moments to bring Him glory and set you free in the midst of it all!

At the end of 1 Timothy, Paul writes something to Timothy that I want to also challenge you with because it resonated in my heart so deeply when I read it.

O Timothy, guard the deposit entrusted to you. Avoid the irreverent babble and contradictions of what is falsely called "knowledge" for by professing it some have swerved from the faith. Grace be with you.
1 Timothy 6:20, ESV

I don't know about you, but I feel the weight of that verse in my life. We have been given the Word of God, time, callings, friendships, relationships, hearts, and bodies to guard as we live out the gospel.

I will never forget one time in college when my best friend and I decided to see what was inside a tennis ball. She played tennis, so one night, we sat in her room with too much time on our hands and decided to cut one of her tennis balls open. We used a butter knife, and with every swipe of that dull blade, we eventually cut that thing open. It was a memory we will never forget (I am still shocked we didn't catch our dorm on fire). Rebekah is one of those friends that always made me feel like I could do anything. She encouraged me at all times. I can't

By Guarding What You've Been Given

think of a time in our almost thirty years of friendship when she made me feel like I couldn't do what God had called me to do. She was always all in, and she was always ready to do something crazy with me. She is still that same person in my life.

I named my Rebekah after her. That's how much I adore her.

How she has been for me made me think about you, the girl or woman holding this book. Are you curious about the things no one cares about? Are you the tired mom longing for your season to change? Are you that college girl who is ready for God to show you what your next steps are?

I promise He sees you. I wrote this book with YOU in mind.

Are you ready?

Are you ready to no longer let every day be set to the rhythm of what you don't have or what you can't do? Are you prepared to lay down your pride and admit you need Jesus to help you? Are you ready to open up God's Word with fresh eyes to see God and who He is and not what you can get from Him? Are you ready to change the world?

I believe with my whole heart God has positioned us in this place in history to go and make disciples of all nations. I believe God has given you precisely what you need through His son, Jesus, to live a FREE and FULL life, regardless of the hard things that come our way.

I want to say thank you for finishing this book and for coming alongside my ADHD brain for the first seven and a half chapters. We now get to move forward together, still processing and wrestling, while choosing to dig deep into God's Word.

Let's go win some battles because we have an advantage, and His name is JESUS!!

Protect What You Cherish

CHAPTER 9

Just one more thing.

My family loves Disney. If you see me traveling in an airport, you'll see a red sequin Minnie Mouse backpack. I will pull a Minnie Mouse suitcase behind me, and if you watch me open my purse to get my cell phone out, you'll see a Minnie Mouse phone case. I am always looking for one more thing Minnie to have, and it's like I can never have enough. It makes me smile and causes me to think about every vacation and fun moment I have ever had at Disney—one more thing.

Have you ever finished a conversation and thought I would have said this or that? What about the argument with that person or even that sweet conversation at a coffee shop? I feel that way today. We need one more conversation, so that's where this chapter came from—one more thing.

When I finished writing, it was like something ignited in me. I don't even know what it is. It's more like a full stomach feeling. I am overwhelmed by God's hand in this journey. I am humbled by the amount of sweet words from the people who know me intimately. I am blown away by the people God has connected me to in the process.

Today feels like one of those days; I just feel hopeful. Remember when you were kids, and you could tag someone to be it? Well, that is my prayer for you.

I want to reach through the book and say, TAG YOU'RE IT.

Now.
Not tomorrow, but today.

Today, you are beautiful.
Today, you are loved.
Today, you are worthy.
Today, you are gifted.
Today, you have what you need.
Today, you have been forgiven.

Today starts right now.

In the story of Ehud, my eyes always shift back over these words.

Ehud escaped while they delayed and he passed beyond the idols and escaped to Seirah.
Judges 3:26

He passed beyond the idols.

He didn't pause, hesitate, or second guess. Nope, he escaped and got out of there. Imagine if he would have hung around. That wouldn't have ended well. Today, some of you need to get back to the words God has called you to be passing by the very idols that keep catching your eye and causing you to slow down. That idol you're bowing down to won't bring you what you're searching for.

Comparison is an idol when it causes you to change who you are or keeps your attention and affection on someone else other than God.

Sexuality is an idol when it causes you to feed that desire, even when it's in direct opposition to God's Word. Stop trying to feed what God has called you to let go of.

Porn is an idol when it causes you to desire it more than your spouse.

By Guarding What You've Been Given

That friendship is an idol if it causes you to become jealous or mad when you're not with them.

That gifting is an idol if it is how you measure success or your worth.

That sport can become your idol when you value it more than prioritizing church.

Not all of those things I listed are bad, but when anything or anyone takes all your affection, time, or money, it's an idol, and you need to keep going and not glance in its direction any longer.

Fear not. I am with you.
Psalm 43:5a, ESV

Really, that's all we need to know. That in all the seeking, guarding, and protecting, God is with us. He has promised to be with us. My love for bears never subsides. Watching videos of them on the internet and hoping and praying I get to see wild bears is one of my favorite things to do. The thrill of seeing a wild bear is so fun to me. Will I get eaten by a bear one day? I hope not, but it's the constant reminder when I see a bear that God has called me to protect what I cherish regardless of my season.

I have recently been reminded of my calling and the authority of God over my calling. He used a feather lying in the bathroom at Fort Caswell to spark something in me. He not only drew my eyes to it, but He has taken me on a whole new journey of settling into what He has called me to, and it's been so exciting. Birds are everywhere, but in the most random God-wink ways; He reminded me of freedom while finishing this book.

He brought my entire passion and calling full circle, and I am smiling as I type this, with tears in my eyes yet again.

So, if there is one more thing I can encourage you, it is to open your eyes. Open your eyes to God's way. His way feels like the best roller coaster, but even more than that, because one day, when we get off, we walk into heaven, and it will all be worth it. Every twist. Every turn. Every drop. Every slow start and bump in the middle of the ride.

It will be worth it.

Jesus is worth it, and He makes you worth it.

By Guarding What You've Been Given

Protect What You Cherish

Bibliography

1. "Jackie Hill Perry Quote - Guard Your Heart Like Your Life Depends... | Quote Catalog," n.d., https://quotecatalog.com/quote/jackie-hill-perry-guard-your-hear-P7vKzgp.

2. Merriam-Webster, s.v."Protect (verb)," accessed July 25, 2024, https://www.merriam-webster.com/dictionary/protect#:~:text=1,%3A%20defend%20sense%201c.

3. Merriam-Webster, s.v. "Cherish (verb)," accessed July 25, 2024, https://www.merriam-webster.com/dictionary/cherish#:~:text=%3A%20to%20keep%20or%20cultivate%20with,the%20mind%20deeply%20and%20resolutely.

4. Merriam-Webster, s.v. "Guard (noun)," accessed July 25, 2024, https://www.merriam-webster.com/dictionary/guard#:~:text=Synonyms%20of%20guard-,1,were%20posted%20around%20the%20camp.

5. The Fugitive (Warner Bros., 1993), https://www.amazon.com/Fugitive-Harrison-Ford/dp/B001EBYM8A.

6. "Jesuit Resource - Black History Month Quotes," n.d. https://www.xavier.edu/jesuitresource/online-resources/quote-archive1/black-history-month-quotes.

7. Erin Fitzgerald, "Bear Hibernation: 5 Fun Facts," Yellowstone Forever, January 20, 2023, https://www.yellowstone.org/bear-hibernation-5-fun-facts/.

8. "Lazy," in Merriam-Webster Dictionary, July 16, 2024, https://www.merriam-webster.com/dictionary/

lazy#:~:text=%3A%20disinclined%20to%20activity%20or%20exertion,a%20lazy%20summer%20day.

9. Cappiello, Julie. "5 Cool Facts About Bears." World Animal Protection US, October 7, 2023, https://www.worldanimalprotection.us/latest/blogs/5-facts-about-bears/.

10. "Knit Together - Vine's Expository Dictionary of NT Words -," StudyLight.org, n.d., https://www.studylight.org/dictionaries/eng/ved/k/knit-together.html.

11. Cambridge Dictionary, s.v. "Unbearable (adjective)," July 24, 2024, https://dictionary.cambridge.org/us/dictionary/english/unbearable.

12. "What Is Sanctification? Bible Definition and Meaning," Bible Study Tools, n.d., https://www.biblestudytools.com/dictionary/sanctification/#:~:text=Baker's%20Evangelical%20Dictionary%20of%20Biblical,use%20intended%20by%20its%20designer.

Holly Myers is a speaker, author, and church leader based in Gastonia, NC. She and her husband, Richard, lead Revolution Church in west Gastonia, where they love building a welcoming community of people who are passionate about living out their faith. Holly and Richard have two daughters, Rachel and Rebekah, and a son-in-law, Austin, who are all a big part of her world.

Holly's heart is in ministry, especially when it comes to pouring into young women. She loves helping girls discover who they are in Christ and walking alongside them as they grow in their faith. With a deep love for God's Word, Holly is all about mentoring and encouraging women in their journey with the Lord.

Outside of church, Holly's favorite things include coffee dates with friends, traveling (Disney is always a win!), and embracing her love for bears, and the smell of skunk. She's passionate about friendship and believes in the power of finding community—something that's a huge part of both her personal and ministry life. Holly's all about building authentic connections and making life's journey more fulfilling with those you love.

Holly Myers
www.hollyhmyers.com